Also by Brian Nolan

HERO: The True Story of the Legendary Canadian Fighter Ace,
Buzz Beurling

King's War

Mackenzie King
and the
Politics of War
1939 - 1945

Brian Nolan

RANDOM HOUSE
TORONTO

Published in Canada in 1988 by Random House of Canada Limited, Toronto.

Canadian Cataloguing in Publication Data
Nolan, Brian
  King's war : Mackenzie King and the politics
of war, 1939–1945

ISBN 0-394-22036-6

1. Canada — Politics and government — 1935–1948.*
2. Canada — History — 1939–1945.* 3. World War,
1939–1945 — Canada. 4. King, William Lyon
Mackenzie, 1874–1950. I. Title.

FC582.N65 1988   971.063′2   C88-094477-3
F1034.N65 1988

The publishers wish to thank the following for permission to reproduce extended extracts from material to which they hold the copyright: Canada's Wings, Inc., *No Reason Why* by Carl Vincent; Collins Publishers, *A World in Flames* by Richard S. Malone; Longmans, Green and Company, *The Incredible Canadian* by Bruce Hutchison; The Macmillan Company of Canada Limited, *A Party Politician* by C.G. Power; McClelland and Stewart Limited, *Duplessis* by Conrad Black and *Mitch Hepburn* by Neil McKenty; Oxford University Press, *Mackenzie King of Canada* by Reginald H. Hardy; Stoddart Publishing, *Tug of War* by W. Denis and Shelagh Whitaker.

Jacket design: Brant Cowie/Artplus Limited
Jacket illustration: Al Wilson

Printed and bound in Canada.

To Cathy, Philip, Mike and Paul

CONTENTS

PART IV, THE FINAL CRISIS
September 1944–December 1944

ACKNOWLEDGEMENTS

Writing books and making films is not unlike going to war. The outcome is never assured until the last word has been spoken or the final frame exposed. In either case the writer or the producer, contrary to popular wisdom, seldom works alone. Such was the case in preparing *King's War*; many helping hands were extended to the author throughout this project. For the research I relied on previously published accounts, identified in the bibliography section, as well as oral history interviews. In regard to the latter category I am sincerely grateful to Cameron Graham, of the Canadian Broadcasting Corporation, and his associate, Nicole Latreille, who allowed me access to their extensive archives in Ottawa, particularly to the file of interviews recorded in the early 1970s for the seven-part documentary television series entitled *The Days Before Yesterday*. Over the years, Mr. Graham's unit has produced a complete cinematic record of Canda's exciting political history from Laurier to Trudeau. Part of that record was *The Days Before Yesterday*, which was first broadcast on the network in the fall of 1973. Literally hundreds of film interviews were conducted in the preparation of the series, and specifically for the period from 1939 to 1945. Since I had worked on *The Days Before Yesterday* as a writer and director, I realized how valuable this archival record was that had been compiled by Mr. Graham and his staff. When I approached him for permission to use this material, Mr. Graham responded with generosity, opening his files for my research. The interviews for the series were conducted between 1970 and 1973 by a number of people including David Scrivens, Robert McKenzie, Geoff Scott, the author, and Mr. Graham himself. The bulk of the several hundred interviews, however, were carried out by two skilful interviewer-researchers, Jean Bruce and Larry Zolf. To all of them, I express my deepest appreciation. Much of the material gathered by these researchers was never used in the finished programs because of the unique restraints imposed by documentary film-making techniques. Nevertheless, there remained a vast well of recollection, and these recordings chiefly comprise the oral component of *King's War*.

I am equally grateful to Donald Brittain and Adam Symansky, of the National Film Board, who also allowed me access to the considerable research they assembled for their six-hour mini-series drama, *The King Chronicle*, which premiered on the CBC in March 1988. Having access to their material in the initial stages of research was also most valuable and time saving.

My thanks also to the respective staffs of Shirley Leishman Books Ltd., of Ottawa, and the Ottawa Public Library, especially the Carlingwood Branch, who went out of their way to obtain a number of volumes which, while still in print, remain difficult to locate, and for their suggestions in tracking down works that are now out of print.

While it is not possible to list everyone who helped me, I would like to mention Bill O'Farrell, Dave Weil, Aileen Cox, Jeff Street, Peter Trueman, and Tony Stachiw, all of whom inexplicably emerged at the precise moment when I needed certain background material. Also I'm indebted to Maureen Stone and Flo Smyth for their diligence in processing the manuscript, and to Ed Carson and Doug Pepper at Random House for their advice and encouragement. Last but certainly not least I thank Vivian, my wife, for her limitless patience and understanding throughout the entire project.

AUTHOR'S NOTE

Although this book examines Mackenzie King as Canada's wartime prime minister, it is neither a biography nor a military history. Both subjects have been exhaustively explored. Readers in search of the definitive biography of King or a chronological accounting of Canadian battles of World War II are therefore advised to look elsewhere.

This is the story of a peculiarly gifted Canadian and the men around him who either supported King's leadership or vigorously challenged it throughout the uncertain days of the war. The events I have chosen to feature, and the structure I have adopted, is entirely subjective.

All quotes are identified either in the text or in the source notes. Interpretation of the King record, when not attributed or identified, is the author's.

Brian Nolan
The Homestead
West Quebec
June, 1988

Mackenzie King genuinely believed and
frequently said that the real secret of
political leadership was more in what was
prevented than what was accomplished.
J.W. Pickersgill

Prologue

The Uncrowned King
of Canada

A S A POLITICIAN HE was called slimy, repulsive, shifty, devious, tricky, cunning, unprincipled, a chameleon, a toad and Machiavelli's Prince. As a person, he was remembered as baffling, weird, mystical, dull, dour and boring. Complicating the portrait, he was known in private to be charming and witty, candid to the point of embarrassment; a pathetic bachelor who frequently and disconsolately fell in love with a succession of women, but who never married. He was also a glutton, wolfing food like some marauding Viking, washing it down with vintage wine. He loved luxury and comfort but most of all power, a fact reflected in his record of 7,829 days of political reign. He held public office longer than any other politician in the English-speaking world. He had been around so long people forgot that he was born in an earlier century when men-at-arms still battled with sabres and warriors fought with bows and arrows. Indeed, only two years after his birth in 1874, George

1

Armstrong Custer, the American cavalry general, was scalped at the hands of Sioux fighters south of the Saskatchewan border in the wind-swept coulees of Montana. Yet, by the time he died in 1950, con-temporary warriors were dispatching their enemies from the face of the earth with thermal energy, leaving the victims' bodies imprinted in X-ray outlines in the dust of Hiroshima and Nagasaki.

Nearly forty years have passed since the death of this extraordinary politician. More extraordinary, four decades later William Lyon Mac-kenzie King has defied analysis, remaining a puzzle. Except for a handful of intimate friends, few really knew him; even fewer loved him. When he died, thousands of Canadians shuffled past his bier on Parliament Hill, but for the most part they remained tearless. They had come to pay final respects but appeared more as curiosity seekers than mourners. For twenty-one years the pale, wasted figure in the coffin had dominated the lives of Canadians and the political fortunes of a nation; six of those years were during the catastrophic days of World War II. In death as in life, King remained a genuine paradox, a contradictory character more mystical than any of his successors. In power he had been cold and distant. While King commanded an army of supporters, his admirers wouldn't have made up a platoon. The handful who claimed to be on intimate terms with him have all remained resolutely vague, thus magnifying the legend. Adding fuel to the burning fire that is the riddle of Mackenzie King, his own voluminous private writings and memoranda have formed the basis of numerous interpretations of his life and work.

Some of the recollections of his life and deeds came in sanitized editions from the partisan pens of steadfast Liberals, political admirers and sycophants eager to perpetuate King's memory as a great inter-national statesman, which he wasn't, or as a wizard politician, at which, in the worst and best definitions of the word, he was unrivalled. King understood that effective leadership, simply put, meant retaining power at any price. This he did with quiet fanaticism during the conscription crisis of the 1940s, a calculated toss of the political dice that caused tragic results on Europe's battlefields for thousands of Canadians who had volunteered to fight in the front lines. To King, there was a greater victory to be won: the survival of the Canadian nation. To avoid the painful and bloody discord that had poisoned the country over the same issue in World War I, King placated Quebec with a series of masterful manoeuvres until he could no longer delay the moment of truth. In the end, he betrayed French Canada and ordered conscripts to the battlefields. It made little difference. Victory was already in sight. By delaying the decision throughout most of the war, King failed to unify the country's quarrelsome racial factions, but he succeeded in preventing either one from precipitous action that in his mind could have led to the dismemberment of confederation. This was the King legacy. ''Mackenzie King genuinely believed and frequently said that the real secret of political leadership was more in what was prevented than what was accomplished,'' remembered J.W. Pickersgill in summing up his boss's matchless political cunning.[1]

Most of what we know about King came from his own expansive diary that he began in 1893. With few exceptions (the year 1913 being one), King made daily entries throughout his life almost until the day he died. Anyone reading the diaries is struck by the amount of detail and trivia that King included in his daily accounts. They suggest to readers that he devoted a disproportionate amount of time recording the banal, and pose the question how he got any other work done. The answer is contained in the diaries. King was indefatigable.

The most comprehensive works to emerge since King's death were *The Mackenzie King Record* (1939–1944) by Pickersgill, and three subsequent volumes (1944–1948) that he co-authored with D.F. Forster, a University of Toronto professor. Pickersgill was quick to point out the work presented King's public life, not his private life, and that no effort was made to write the ''history of his times or to present views of his contemporaries.''[2] The result was a fascinating account of history as told by Mackenzie King in the form of uncontested testimony. The role of the critic fell to other writers, journalists and historians, notably C.P. Stacey, who examined King's strange, private world, unpeeling the layers of his eccentric personality. Canadians were shocked, intrigued, even titillated as the details of the private King were made public. Other Canadians were simply left baffled as to how this bizarre figure had functioned at all. The more they read about King, the more he took on the grotesque shape of a Jekyll and

Hyde double. Most alarming, though, there was nothing fictional about Mackenzie King. He communicated through mediums with the dead —departed spirits who talked to him through a silver trumpet. After the war, long after Hitler had blown his brains out in his Berlin bunker, the dead dictator appeared to King in a vision. King considered his pet dog a saint, the living embodiment of his mother and Jesus Christ. Had King shown up at the admitting ward of any psychiatric hospital, especially in the 1930s, even the most junior of interns would have wondered whether the man was certifiable.

Naturally, the tantalizing question is raised: to what extent was King influenced in his decisions by his occult world? The answer has bedevilled all writers who have poked into this strange compartment of King's personality. H. Blair Neatby's conclusion seemed to convince most other investigators. "Mackenzie King was influenced by the unseen world to the extent that when he had spiritual confirmation he was less likely to be swayed by mortal colleagues. When the voices did not confirm his own judgment, they were truly immaterial."[3]

Walter Turnbull, who served King as a principal secretary for nine years, said King "consulted spiritual advisers in the way that you and I take advice. We only look for that kind of advice that we want to hear, and when we don't get it, we reject it. So, if the spirit world told him this was fine, he thought this was a good sign, and when it didn't tell him what he wanted to hear, he said this was just superstitious nonsense."[4] Nonsense indeed, said Joy E. Esberey, a political scientist, in her engrossing study of King, *Knight of the Holy Spirit*. "It contributes nothing to our understanding of King to draw a sharp line between his private world, dominated by his interest in the survival of the human spirit, and his public world of practical politics," she wrote. Nor was it, Esberey said, accurate to portray King "as an individual struggling to maintain two separate levels of existence, one worldly and one other-wordly."[5] Esberey concluded that while King was neurotic, his pronounced neurosis did not impair his leadership.

Joan Patteson, who spent many a night with King at the "table," was greatly disturbed when the Duchess of Hamilton, another of King's many séance partners, wrote after his death that King "fully appreciated the spiritual direction of the universe and was always seeking guidance for himself in his work."[6] Patteson was so upset she wrote to Violet Markham, a wealthy British aristocrat and friend of King, to refute the Duchess's published account. "Never did he allow his belief to enter into his public life," Patteson was quoted as saying.[7] Stacey, who produced the exhaustive study of King's personal life, said the "spirits did not in general tell him what to do. They told him that what he had done, or what he had decided to do, was right. Thus they sent him on his way with confidence renewed."[8]

All these facets of King's private world lay hidden behind his bland exterior. There must have been hundreds of people who were aware of his strange behaviour, yet the public never learned of his aberrations until after his death. While he was alive, Canadians were puzzled how this nondescript individual survived with so little visible talent in the precarious profession of politics. In the age of television and Kennedy charisma, King would have probably failed miserably. A terrible orator, his flat, monotonous voice put to sleep friend and foe alike, whether in the Commons, over radio or on the hustings. His speeches were unmemorable. He droned on interminably; his sentences were convoluted and their meaning nearly always ambiguous. This, of course, was to his advantage. It was seldom that anyone, including his staff and colleagues, knew exactly what he meant, which suited King. He could never be accused of having said anything, earning him one of the most damning printable epithets in Canadian politics. Frank Scott, poet and defender of civil liberties, said this of King: "Truly he will be remembered wherever men honor ingenuity, ambiguity, inactivity and political longevity."[9]

One of King's apologist biographers admitted, "King operated mainly on the principle that the fewer definite promises one makes the less trouble one gets into." H. Reginald Hardy added, "Such ambiguous statements provided King with convenient fire-exits in case of emergency. These were always left unbolted and they opened freely on well-oiled hinges."[10]

A reformer in his early career who championed the downtrodden and the underdog in public, King pursued a private life of comfort and luxury. Always impeccably tailored, he was as fastidious about his dress as he was about the preparation of his food. King delighted in giving intimate dinner parties, fussing over the menu like a head waiter, seeing that only correct vintages were served, even writing the guests' names on the place cards himself, a habit he picked up from Sir Wilfrid Laurier, whom King worshipped. "King thought that it was a thoughtful gesture," said Hardy.[11] Yet he could be thoughtless in a cavalier manner. All during the 1930s when thousands of victims of depression Canada trudged lonely roads, hitch-hiked and rode the rails, King travelled first class in chauffeured limousines, luxuriously appointed steamship cabins and aboard mahogany-panelled private railway cars. When wartime demanded less opulent modes of transport, King tempered his tastes, but not significantly.

He sought the good life and the ways of the wealthy, frequently a guest of the Rockefellers and the Roosevelts. David Rockefeller recalled "numerous occasions" when King visited the Rockefeller mansion at 10 West 54th Street in New York City, as well bunking in at the sprawling family home in Seal Harbor, Maine.[12] The King-Rockefeller friendship began in the coalfields of Colorado during World War I. King had been hired by John D. Rockefeller, Jr., in 1915 to bring harmony between miners and one of Rockefeller's numerous companies, Colorado Fuel and Iron. Rockefeller had heard of King's record as a conciliator in settling forty industrial disputes while serving as Canada's young deputy minister of labour at the turn of the century. After the Ludlow Massacre, in which protesting miners, women and children were shot by the state militia, Rockefeller was in need of urgent advice. King succeeded in obtaining an agreement between Colorado Fuel and Iron and the company's 12,000 workers — a settlement that endeared King to the heart of the aloof U.S. tycoon. Years later, David, his son, said, "Father had no one in his life he considered to be a better friend than Mr. King."[13] It was a friendship Rockefeller later cemented with a personal gift of $100,000 to King in his twilight years, which partly explains why King to the end always addressed Rockefeller as mister.

Throughout his life King was a familiar figure at Franklin Roosevelt's always noisy and bustling homestead at Hyde Park, N.Y. Their only apparent link was that both were graduates of Harvard. Curiously, other than being leaders of their respective countries, they shared little in common. King, while maintaining a liking for good wine, usually limited his hard liquor intake to one drink. He was also a non-smoker. Still, King tolerated F.D.R., who puffed thirty Camels a day, drank numerous straight-up martinis any time and kept a mistress full time. Yet they remained fast friends and King was frequently invited to the White House and the president's Georgia retreat at Warm Springs.

King's taste for the aristocratic life was in contrast to the image he presented to his neighbours in Ottawa's Sandy Hill district as the guy next door taking his dog out for a walk before bedtime. Always, there were two Kings: the prim politician and the bachelor "catlike in his love for comfort."[14] King found that comfort in two permanent residences: Kingsmere, the 500-acre country estate in the Gatineau Hills of Quebec across the Ottawa River; and Laurier House, a spooky-looking Victorian mansion in Sandy Hill.

Laurier House was quite haunted by the memory of King's mother and other visions, voices and apparitions who appeared and spoke to King throughout his life. King, who idolized his mother, kept a table lamp burning in the house as a vigil so that it cast surrealistic light on a life-size portrait of Mrs. King.

King's life was dominated by his mother. It has been chronicled that he never married simply because he could not find a woman to match the qualities of Isabel King. Yet the search for the ideal woman was lifelong and ended in failure. In his youth, King sought the companionship of prostitutes but most of his other many relationships were, apparently, Platonic. There was Violet Markham and Julia Grant, the granddaughter of President Ulysses S. Grant. But all these passionate affairs, conducted mostly through the mails, were for naught. The only one that may not have been Platonic involved the darkly attractive wife of the manager of Molson's Bank in Ottawa. Mary Joan MacWhirther Patteson and her husband, Godfroy, were neighbours in Ottawa at the Roxborough apartments where King lived in 1918. Ronald Blumer, in preparing the research-scenario for the TV mini-series on the life of King for the National Film Board and CBC-TV, speculated this way: "It was all very Platonic until 1921 when things came to a crisis. Joan and King began to get closer and closer until . . . we don't know. King who saved every scrap of paper in his life, including a lot of embarrassing stuff, cut these key five-and-a-half pages out of his diary. When we return King is praying in his boathouse at Kingsmere for forgiveness."[15] Whatever happened, Patteson became a lifelong friend, an unofficial first-lady-in-hiding who offered counsel to the bachelor prime minister to the end. After 1933 she joined him in frequent séances "over the 'little table', those voyages into what he called the beyond. . . ."[16] As these hidden details emerged, they served only to whet the public appetite, since Canadians remembered King in his final years as a short (he was five feet, six and a half inches) old man waddling across the snowy expanses of Parliament Hill in a bowler hat and coonskin coat. But in his youth, King was handsome and athletic, a perfect model of the muscular Christian, plunging into cold, northern rivers for a swim, or running through back-lit forests on the university harrier team. King presented an attractive figure when he first burst upon the Ottawa social scene at the turn of the century as an eligible and charming bachelor, quite the opposite picture he projected as a civil servant, member of Parliament and later as prime minister. Pickersgill recalled King as a "marvellous host and excellent company" at his intimate dinner parties.[17] Malcolm MacDonald, the U.K. High Commissioner, remembered King as very convivial, personally waiting on his guests. "He was a host, not prime minister. And this was a charming side of his character which many people never saw," said MacDonald.[18] King's charms were not reserved only for diplomats. In the Colorado coalfields, he won the heart of "Mother" Jones, a tough he-man feminist who spoke for the miners, and the respect of Samuel Gompers, the legendary U.S. union and labour leader.

Women, though, were his special target. "King's tremendous asset was the way he could charm women, any age," said James Sinclair, the Liberal M.P. for Vancouver North, and father of Margaret Trudeau-Kemper.[19] Sinclair recalled a meeting between King and Pat Gibson, the wife of Jack Gibson, an independent member of Parliament for Comox-Alberni. When they parted, Pat blurted out: "Mr. King, how is it that such a wonderful man like yourself never married?" King, in Sinclair's recollection, took her by the arm and replied: "My dear, if I'd met a girl like you forty years ago, I would be married."[20]

While King was capable of laying on the blarney in private, his demeanour in public was dour. The only joke King ever uttered publicly that anyone remembered involved Doukhobors. W.K. ''Billy'' Esling, the Conservative member for Kootenay West, asked in the House, ''What would the Prime Minister do, I should like to know, if one evening he discovered three Doukhobor women in his garden?'' In a flash, King jumped to his feet. ''I should send for the leaders of the opposition,'' he shot back, amidst laughter, knowing that leaders of the opposition parties were both bachelors like himself.[21]

There was, however, little humour in his day-to-day life. A demanding boss, King was insensitive to the feelings of his staff, frequently calling on them at any time of day or night, holidays or weekends, to take on some churlish assignment. ''All industry and no humanity,'' joked Pickersgill, referring to King's book, *Industry and Humanity*, published in 1918,[22] his personal blueprint for improving society's lot. Yet, those who observed him at close range remembered more than just a selfish, vain and thoughtless person. ''For every story of neglect or forgetfulness, there were a half dozen [other stories] to refute such testimony,'' said Reginald Hardy.[23] He remembered how King once appeared as a simple mourner in the funeral procession of two children who had died in a fire in Ottawa's Lower Town.

The stories about King grew with each passing decade, some of them plausible, others preposterous. No figure in Canadian politics, save Trudeau perhaps, was the object of so much praise, condemnation and vilification; he was the subject of tales and yarns that in the end created the oddest of all Canadian legends. While many could describe King, no one could define him; he had spent a lifetime weaving his own impenetrable cloak of mystery. This he wore to his grave.

In the summer of 1939, Canadians did not possess all the facts about Mackenzie King that historians and psychologists, supporters and opponents, apologists and chronologists have amassed since his death. His failure to recognize the meaning of rising fascism was colossal, his belief that Canada could isolate itself from this black menace, disastrous. "The first and gravest failure of his life," said Bruce Hutchison of this blunder to understand the world's drift to war and anarchy.[24] When the war clouds finally broke, some Canadians certainly doubted whether this bland, vacillating politician was capable of leading Canada to victory. Moreover, this same man who, if in fact but not in title, would become the commander-in-chief, was not only lacking in military training but was suspected of dodging service in World War I. The charge was unfair since King was forty years old when World War I began. During the 1930 election campaign, King was asked why he hadn't served in World War I. He explained that his commitments at the time were to his ailing mother and his sickly brother, Macdougall. Besides, he told the delegates, he hadn't been altogether well himself at the time, a response which inspired a heckler to shout, "Did you have dandruff?"[25] Yet this was the man who stood before Canadians that last summer of peace before the war to lead them through their darkest hour. George S. Patton, America's manic battlefield commander, said that to win wars it takes men who are simple, direct and ruthless. Mackenzie King was hardly simple, certainly never direct. As the war ground on, a few of King's friends and all of his enemies learned in varying degrees, some to their everlasting regret, the depth of ruthlessness of Canada's wartime prime minister. What Canadians didn't know, and had no way of knowing, was that their leader saw himself as some kind of northern Mahdi, a prophet anointed by the Almighty to save the world and rid it of evil. For six years, Canada would fall in behind the least likely person, by any standard, to be judged a fanatic, a man with a divine mission.

Prelude

The Divine Mission

THEY MADE THE ODDEST of couples. The host wore white tie and tails, appearing more as a band leader than the chancellor of Germany. His guest, in pin-striped grey pants and morning coat, looked for all the world like a floor-walker in a fashionable department store, not the prime minister of Canada.

Mackenzie King met Adolf Hitler June 29, 1937, a warm, overcast Tuesday in Berlin, a fleeting moment in history that was later described as "one of the most bizarre episodes in the short and rather sedative history of Canadian external affairs."[1] King had been mulling over such a meeting for at least a year, trying out the idea on Prime Minister Baldwin of Britain who, for whatever reason, didn't think much of the suggestion. Still, King persisted and when the moment of opportunity presented itself, he moved. He had just attended the Imperial Conference of 1937 and the coronation of George VI, a man who gained instant sympathy in the heart of Mackenzie King and someone who no doubt gave him additional inspiration to proceed with his unusual mission. A shy figure with a stutter, George displayed a deep sense of duty to the throne that his weak and confused brother,

Edward VIII, had not demonstrated. His abdication the year before
to marry Wallis Warfield Simpson, an American, was necessary, as
Edward told a global radio audience, because the heavy burdens of
kingship were intolerable "without the help and support of the woman
I love."[2] Edward's abdication was just another depressing event in a
gloomy world being crushed by economic misery, and worse, rapidly
spreading fascism. Doubtless, the new monarch's quiet display of courage infused King with renewed hope as much as it did the common
man.

While George VI reconciled the differences within the House of
Windsor, King saw the time ripe for a greater reconciliation, this
between the West and an increasingly nationalistic Germany. Like any
odyssey, King's was not without apprehension and mishap. In Paris
en route, as ridiculous as it sounds, the prime minister of Canada had
trouble cashing a cheque. After fretting and fuming, King got cash
and made the Gare du Nord for the 7:15 P.M. night train to Berlin
where, upon his arrival the next morning, he checked into the swanky
Adlon Hotel, forgoing an invitation to stay at the British Embassy as
guest of Sir Nevile Henderson, the recently appointed British ambassador. Henderson, like so many others, had misread King's obstinate
personality—this was to be King's own summit. He was well ahead
of his time in applying this innovative diplomacy. As events transpired,
none of the leading Allied war chieftains — Stalin, Churchill and
Roosevelt—ever met Hitler face to face. Only King achieved this.
What Hitler thought about King is not known but unfortunately the
impression Hitler left on the Canadian "distorted all King's thinking
on the human tragedy now about to open."[3]

In King's defence, an understanding of the times is necessary. He
found himself suddenly transported to the very heart of Hitler's social
revolution. Compared to the Canada King had just left, a land of
drought and crippling unemployment, with a million men, women and
children being fed massive government relief, the leafy capital of the
New Germany seemed a Babylon, its insouciance palpable. Berliners
were the New Yorkers of Europe, sassy, confident and always slightly
cynical. Their tastes for pleasurable restaurants and sophisticated theatre were varied and demanding.

In contrast to the rural Canada of outhouses, kerosene lamps and one-furrow ploughs, the Germans were radically changing their country's landscape. Under construction was the autobahn, a multi-lane freeway designed to carry a revolutionary automobile dubbed "the people's car." (It became the original VW Beetle.) Since coming to power four years previously, Hitler had already re-employed six million Germans from the jobless ranks of the Depression, raised standards of housing and health, and probably more significantly, instilled a renewed pride in themselves that erased the guilt of the Great War. Who would not have been impressed? Certainly, King was.

The glittering prosperity, however, also served to hide Germany's darker record since Hitler became chancellor in 1933; there were sinister events that even the most gullible visitor could hardly ignore. The Führer had already withdrawn Germany from the League of Nations and had stunned his own countrymen with the wholesale murders of his troublesome Brownshirts which some historians say totalled nearly 200. Over a two-day period in the early summer of 1934, they had been rounded up in a purge the press called "The Night of the Long Knives" and systematically eliminated. Later, explaining the purge to the deputies of the Reichstag, which should have served as a portent of things to come, Hitler said: "The Supreme Court of the German people during these twenty-four hours consisted of myself!"[4] Less than a month after the domestic blood-letting, the Nazis murdered Engelbert Dollfuss, the Austrian Chancellor. By March 1935, Hitler had decreed universal military service for all Germans and, a year later, marched some of them into the Rhineland. Running parallel to these disturbing developments, Mussolini had invaded Ethiopia in the uneven match of tanks against tribesmen's spears. If all of these things were not enough to make a visitor stop and ponder, there was the Spanish Civil War aflame on the Iberian Peninsula, already a year into its misery.

King found himself in the German capital against this backdrop of events, recent history which surely should have triggered some kind of warning signal in his thoughts. It didn't, and his itinerary, carefully orchestrated by his Nazi hosts, didn't help. Before meeting Hitler, King was subjected to a whirlwind tour of Hitler Youth camps and a visit with the wholesomely tanned young men and women of the Labour Service Corps. The *Arbeitsdienst*, an egalitarian, semi-military organization whose members worked as farm-hands and labourers, were frequently the focus of propaganda newsreels as they marched off to the fields carrying chromium-plated shovels.

King was also whisked to a coffee-klatsch with Hermann Göring, the corpulent and most gregarious of Hitler's top Nazis. Göring, in an immaculately pressed white Luftwaffe general's uniform, was all charm and grace, thanking King for six bison that Canada had sent to the Berlin Zoo, and expressing interest in visiting the Rockies to do some big game hunting himself. King extended an open invitation to Göring, then departed to meet with Hitler. The Führer arranged to see King at the old palace of Paul von Hindenburg on the Wilhelmstrasse rather than at the chancellery which Hitler said looked more "like the headquarters of a soap company," than the centre of the Reich.[5] The Nazis pulled out all the stops in greeting the Canadian prime minister. Hitler's *Leibstandarte*, the Führer's élite bodyguards, was drawn up to salute the arriving Canadian. While the professionals of the Wehrmacht derisively referred to them as "asphalt soldiers" (they were always goose-stepping around the streets of Berlin), *Leibstandarte* presented as impressive a sight now as they had a year before when they made their public appearance at the Berlin Summer Olympics.

Inside, King was escorted to a second floor reception room where Hitler waited. Impressed by what he had seen for the two previous days, King immediately complimented Hitler on the constructive work of his régime, adding that it was "bound to be followed in other countries to the great advantage of mankind."[6] The meeting, which King had been told would probably last no more than thirty minutes, stretched to an hour and a quarter. King's impressions of Hitler, recalled a half century later, are naïve and embarrassing. If anyone had access to King's diary while he was still in office during the war, its contents, if made public, surely would have spelled political disaster for the most political of all Canada's prime ministers. For the record, these were King's comments:

He smiled very pleasantly and indeed had more a sort of appealing and affectionate look in his eyes. My sizing up of the man as I sat and talked with him was that he is really one who truly loves his fellow-men and his country. . . . His face is much more prepossessing than his picture would give the impression of. It is not that of a fiery over-strained nature but of a calm, passive man, deeply and thoughtfully in earnest. His skin was smooth; his face did not present lines of fatigue or weariness.

His eyes impressed me most of all. There was a liquid quality about them which indicate keen perception and profound sympathy —(calm, composed)—and one could see how particularly humble folk would come to have a profound love for the man. . . .[7]

King of course was not the only Western politician to be charmed by the dictator. Churchill himself once expressed admiration for Hitler for championing Germany's renewed sense of pride in the early 1930s.

King told Hitler that Canada and the Commonwealth would stand by Britain in the event of war. However, until the last hour of peace, King was still telling Canadians that Parliament, and only Parliament, would make the decision whether or not to commit itself to the world conflict. Their meeting ended with the dictator presenting the prime minister with an autographed photo of himself. That night King attended the Berlin opera and was given Hitler's personal box from which to enjoy Verdi's *Masked Ball*, which King found well performed, beautifully rendered and excellently staged. Before retiring, King confided to his diary, "Looking back over the German visit, I can honestly say that it was as enjoyable, informative and inspiring as any visit I have ever had anywhere. . . . I have come away from Germany tremendously relieved. I believe that there will not be war."[8]

Despite an urgent warning beforehand from Violet Markham not to be hypnotized by the evil genius, it was a peculiar relationship that defies understanding fifty years later, and yet one that can be partially explained by the fact both men shared much in common. Although Hitler kept a mistress — Eva Braun, the mixed-up film actress who appeared in German pot-boilers called "mountain pictures"—he, like King, was a confirmed bachelor. Both, too, retained an idealistic image of their mothers. (King later commented on this.) When Hitler's mother

Klara died, the attending doctor who had sat through numerous death-bed scenes said he "never saw anyone so prostrate with grief as Adolf Hitler."[9] Also, the two men were meticulous on matters of their health. Smoking was *verboten*, and they tippled only lightly. In art, their tastes were startlingly similar.

Although King lived through a period of new, explosive artistic energy in Canada he, like Hitler, was a devotee of the "down by the old mill stream" school of art. Hitler considered modern art degenerate. At the opening of Munich's Haus der Deutschen Kunst, three weeks after meeting King, the dictator went into a sulk when he found the jury had rejected a gigantic painting of a man on a hill playing a violin.

The leaders of Canada and Germany had also set down in writing their visions of a better tomorrow. Hitler did so in his *Mein Kampf*, King with his *Industry and Humanity*. Coincidentally, Hutchison described the latter as King's *Mein Kampf*. While *Industry and Humanity*, Hutchison quickly qualified, "was in all respects the antipode of Hitler's work, a Christian challenge to everything Hitler and all other dictators stood for, it parallels Hitler's testament in its basic design."[10]

But the real tie that bound King and Hitler was a spiritual one. Both held unshakable beliefs that Providence had chosen them for great achievement and motivated King's extraordinary visit to Berlin in 1937. As far back as October 1935, King believed he had received his marching orders from the spirits for this divine mission. Lords Oxford and Asquith (Stacey pointed out that King's messages more often than not came from departed Liberal spirits) had assured King, "You will succeed in making peace among the nations of Europe."[11] It was no surprise that on meeting Hitler, King felt he was connecting with a kindred spirit, going as far as to remark that the Führer reminded him of Joan of Arc, and that Hitler was "distinctly a mystic."[12]

Certainly King returned from Germany having made a picture of Hitler in his own image, said Stacey, "embroidering the impressions left in his mind by their one interview, and pushed on by his apparently sincere belief in his divine mission as a peacemaker."[13]

Not long after King's return to Canada, he invited Hutchison to dine alone with him at Laurier House. The writer found King in high spirits and good appetite, attacking a four-course meal and three glasses of vintage white wine with his customary mealtime gusto. While King may have described Hitler as Joan of Arc in his diary, he told Hutchison that he was a "simple sort of peasant," lacking intelligence and of no serious danger to anyone. Hutchison found King "to be a man without a care of any sort," an impression that left the writer disquieted.[14]

As the 1930s rolled to their end, Hitler's instalment-plan acquisition of the European landscape continued unchecked. In March 1936, Hitler had marched into the Rhineland. Now, barely nine months after the King-Hitler summit, and again in the fateful month of March, the grey Nazi war machine swept into Austria where Hitler was greeted with thundering "Sieg Heils!" Surrounded now on three sides, neighbouring Czechoslovakia's fate was sealed, only briefly forestalled by Britain and France giving in to Hitler's next demand to annex the Sudeten area of the country. The appeasement of Hitler by Prime Minister Chamberlain and French Premier Daladier in the infamous Munich Agreement was the falsest of dawns. Throughout these hectic days, although King's influence was minimal, he continued to pursue his divine mission to appeal to the spiritual side of the Führer. At the height of the Munich crisis, King sent a cable to Hitler, perhaps the most cryptic in the history of Canadian diplomacy. Remembering Hitler had remarked in their Berlin meeting that he couldn't think straight in crowded cities, King dashed off the following message: "Get out of Berlin!"[15] There is no record of how Hitler responded to this.

To the very end, however, King remained a supporter of appeasement, sending yet another cable in the wake of Munich to Chamberlain that "the heart of Canada is rejoicing tonight at the success which has crowned your unremitting efforts for peace."[16] In truth, the sentiments did accurately reflect Canada's mood. King, who had no peer when it came to sensing public opinion, was only reflecting the thoughts of Canadians. While King was accused of forcing appeasement and isolationism on the country, it was the opposite that happened. Canada forced isolationism on King. Like millions around the world, Canadians too were deluded that Hitler could be appeased, a belief that was shared by any number of mighty thinkers, including George Bernard Shaw and Gertrude Stein. It was a minority that realized conciliation was not going to work, although John W. Dafoe, the great journalist of the *Winnipeg Free Press*, was one of a handful who did. Members of King's staff, like their boss, remained fervent isolationists almost to the eve of war. Pickersgill himself "thought we should leave the Europeans to stew in their own juice. I couldn't conceive that the Germans could have built up a military machine that could have beat the British and the French. Well, I was just totally wrong but I too was in good company."[17] Hutchison's view was a more critical one. "A greater leader and a greater man, a more brave and a wiser man would have taken the stand then," he said. "I don't think that excuses King's waffling throughout the period, but it explains it."[18]

The last spring of peace arrived on wings of gloom. Six months after Munich, the German army occupied the rest of Czechoslovakia, its youthful soldiers strolling on the cobbles of Wenceslaus Square in Prague while high above the city Adolf Hitler viewed his latest conquest from the steps of Hradshin castle. It was of little solace when Britain finally abandoned appeasement, announcing aid to Poland, which the Führer then coveted.

In Canada, the despair of the times was only slightly dissipated by the arrival in May of George VI and Queen Elizabeth for a nation-wide Royal Tour. It was a visit that cheered Canadians and one that King seemed to personally orchestrate, occasionally to the exclusion of competing politicians. He was everywhere and ever-present, waddling behind the royal couple with his strange duck-like walk, greeting their majesties in his bleating voice at a succession of receptions, fêtes and open-air ceremonies. In June, the King and Queen departed to the tearful singing of *Auld Lang Syne*. Canadians spent the rest of the summer huddled around the radio, hypnotized by Hitler's threatening and pervasive presence.

Even in these dying days of peace, King remained convinced that appeasement still had not failed the world. One last time he contacted Hitler, certain an appeal to the dictator's humanity was still possible. In his reply in July, Hitler invited a "number of Canadian students and officers to visit Germany as a guest of the Third Reich."[19] Even though the invitation arrived amidst Hitler's latest demand, the reunification of the so-called Free City of Danzig with a greater Germany, King was ecstatic. This was proof his divine mission had not failed and that Hitler's invitation was an opportunity "to practise appeasement at the eleventh hour, and to vindicate it in the eyes of its detractors."[20] Not only did King accept the invitation but decided to lead the small delegation personally. James Eayrs said had it departed, "the Prime Minister of Canada, together with a dozen leading Canadians, might have spent the war in an internment camp," a fate King's Tory detractors would have found entirely suitable.[21]

But King's divine mission was an utter failure, its doom heralded by the sound of guns of the German battleship *Schleswig-Holstein* on the morning of September 1, 1939. From the harbour of Danzig, now Gdansk, the old battle wagon lobbed her shells ahead of advancing German soldiers moving stealthily into Polish territory.

To describe King's state of mind as being frantic is not to exaggerate. The evening after war broke out, King and Joan Patteson, holed up at Kingsmere, were in a state of high agitation, "the craziest of all their sessions with the little table," as Stacey described it.[22] The spirits, including his father, mother, Laurier and Gladstone, assured King that Hitler was dead, shot by a Pole. Isabel King was adamant that war was going to be averted. When King came to his senses, he admitted he had been defrauded by this most bizarre of séances, and that it was perfectly clear that a lying spirit intervened.

Devastated by this deceit, King finally turned to the duty at hand: accepting that the inevitable could no longer be avoided. He would lead Canada in its moment of peril, and without benefit of assistance from the occult world. Stacey claimed once war began, King more or less did reject spiritualism for the duration but, like the drinker who has taken the pledge, resorted at intervals to his weakness. King continued to study tea leaves, enjoyed mystical dreams, interpreted the presence of sudden draughts, and forever continued to read significance into the positions of the hands of the clock.

Dismayed but determined, King faced the greatest challenge ever handed to a Canadian prime minister, made more burdensome because of his age. At sixty-five, a time when most men headed into retirement, King inherited the onerous task of leading a nation to war.

His journey would be long and dark, comforted perhaps by the image he held of himself and shared by Violet Markham, who had written long before that "I like to think of you as one of Heine's 'Knights of the Holy Spirit' girt with the sword of justice, truth and purity waging war against all sin and sordidness."[23] This Tennyson ideal of conduct that he adopted remained the greatest of all mysteries about Mackenzie King. As the war darkened, Canadians found out soon enough that his velvet glove of leadership concealed an iron fist; he was a man who without so much as a blink would "cut your throat with a dull knife."[24]

On September 10, 1939, Canada declared hostilities. King's war had begun.

PART I

ENEMIES WITHIN
September 1939–
November 1941

CHAPTER ONE

Treachery in Quebec

OR A MAN WHO lead a sedentary life, Mackenzie King went into battle remarkably fit. Six days after war was declared, George S. McCarthy, his personal physician, called at Laurier House to give King an extensive examination. McCarthy noted the prime minister's blood pressure at 123 over 90 and recorded that his circulation and colour were good, tongue clean, rectum and prostate normal. The results left King feeling as "free as a youngster."[1] McCarthy told King he was generally astounded at his appearance and strength, but was concerned with his weight of 178 pounds and ordered daily exercises. Pat, King's beloved Irish terrier, got a near-clean bill of health from a vet about the same time but, like his master, Pat too was overweight. Both would have to cut down on their bedtime snack of Ovaltine and oatmeal cookies. Still, King noted in his diary that he was "really in good shape to start the work of war."[2] And it was a good thing he was. On September 25, Maurice Duplessis, the premier of Quebec, attacked both King's constitution and his sensibilities by suddenly calling a general election in a month's time. Duplessis cited proclamations made by Ottawa under the War Measures Act as a federal invasion of provincial rights. The day the Wehrmacht crept into Poland that September, the government had put the armed forces on active service, using the all-encompassing WMA as authority to do so. Duplessis charged that Ottawa was encroaching on the freedoms of Quebecers. King, and for that matter, successive Canadian governments regarded the War Measures Act as a convenient piece of legislation to be invoked during tough times. When Duplessis opposed King, the prime minister accused him of being "a second Hitler in his tactics, and methods."[3] More to the point, King was acutely aware of the perilous position Duplessis had placed Ottawa in by attempting to isolate Quebec from the rest of Canada, disrupting the war effort, which was barely moving in low gear, and igniting the smouldering hatred between French and English. King's assessment was that the forthcoming battle in Quebec "would be outstanding in the political history of our Dominion."[4] Just as astutely, King knew Duplessis was a formidable opponent. His reputation as a corrupt demagogue and dictator was one which the Quebec premier had not earned, according to Conrad Black, Duplessis's biographer. While Black describes Duplessis as a fanatical upholder of Parliament, the courts and the rule of law, he "did not hesitate to bend them to his own purposes."[5] This description leaves an observer to ponder what constitutes the definition of a dictator.

Why Duplessis called the snap election is not, even now, entirely clear. His Union Nationale Party was elected in 1936 and still had a year-and-a-half in office. Duplessis said publicly he wanted a new mandate for Quebec's "autonomy," a phrase that sent politicians and academics scrambling for interpretation. Hutchison said, "At least it meant that the provincial government assumed the right to veto the war plans of the Federal Government in Quebec and make a travesty of the constitution."[6] A more plausible explanation, if somewhat convoluted, was the fact that Duplessis was a Conservative at heart. The conscription crisis of Robert Borden's Tory government during World War I had been so destructive that Duplessis achieved power eighteen years later only by calling his rose by another name: the

Union Nationale Party. André Laurendeau concluded that Duplessis sensed King was about to make the same errors and judged the circumstances to be ripe to renew his mandate and to distance himself from the issue that could prove to be politically fatal. Whatever the Liberal King might be forced to do, he, Duplessis the Conservative, was going on the record against conscription.

To King, Duplessis's motives were sinister ones, those of "a thorough gangster."[7]

In truth, Duplessis, like King, was a towering paradox. "Gregarious and aloof, generous and cruel, all-forgiving and vindictive," Duplessis was his own one-man government, and therefore extremely dangerous.[8]

"He believed in doing what had to be done, and he believed in doing it in the quickest way possible," said Tracy S. Ludington, Duplessis's principal public relations adviser in English from 1937 to 1959.[9] "When he walked into a Cabinet meeting, the entire business was in a series of folders under his arm, and he just walked around the table and put everybody's folder in front of them and in that folder it told him exactly what he wanted him to do," recalled Ludington. Duplessis, unlike King, always got to the heart of the matter. Ludington remembers: "I can recall one occasion in which a member of the House said something to him while standing in front of his desk that he didn't like . . . and he just reached over and punched the man in the jaw and the man fell to the floor." Curiously, this pugnacious behaviour masked a deeply held conviction by Duplessis that, like King, he had been called on by Providence to lead his people. "He was a very religious man, you know. *Extremely* religious man," said Ludington. "He not only went to Mass every Sunday, but he went to Mass every Wednesday morning too without exception. No matter where he was, he had to make arrangements to go to Mass Wednesday morning, Wednesday being St. Joseph's Day and St. Joseph being his patron saint. He believed that from somewhere he had received this calling, almost as somebody who received a religious calling to be in the ministry."[10]

Black supports Ludington's thesis, saying Duplessis "believed in only two entities: the Roman Catholic Church and Quebec."[11] These convictions, however, did not deter him from a life of incontinence.

An extremely heavy drinker during most of his life, Duplessis kept a series of mistresses, always in a discreet way. He was more reckless in procuring women for what his associates called his "one-night stands."[12] The processions of painted women coming to the chief's tent was a well known fact. After he died, one of the mistresses, a Mme. Flynn, telephoned Auréa Cloutier, Duplessis's long-time secretary, asking for a small memento of her dead lover. "Madame, I have approved of none of your initiatives," said Mlle. Cloutier, hanging up on the distressed Mme. Flynn.[13]

Women found Duplessis attractive. Black described him: "A distinguished looking man of the mould of the traditional French country haute bourgeoisie, with sharp features, an ample nose, splendid smile, a full head of hair and a slight, well-trimmed moustache."[14] He had recognizably Bourbon features, especially the Bourbon nose, a physical characteristic that became the focus of many cartoonists of the day. Duplessis was average height (five feet, nine inches) and wore clothes tastefully and elegantly. He lived most of his life in two hotel suites, one in the Chateau Frontenac in Quebec City, the other in the Ritz-Carlton in Montreal. They were comfortable if not lavishly furnished lairs, where the lingering aroma of the twenty Larenagas cigars he smoked each day permeated the suites' decorative brocade.

Duplessis was the first of a succession of Canadian politicians to impose a presidential stamp on his office. While it is common enough now to see prime ministers and premiers hurtling through the streets in limousines behind smoked, bullet-proof glass and flag-bedecked fenders, Duplessis long ago had designated his two giant Cadillacs numbers one and two, the same way presidents today mark their jets. In a blatant display of patronage, Duplessis also decreed that additional licence plates numbered 3 through 2000 were to be issued to members of his régime. To remind the recipients who their benefactor was, Duplessis could just as easily revoke the privilege by taking away the plates or demoting an offender from number 52 to 1500. This kind of patronage, condescending though it was, was an accepted fact of Quebec politics, as was the practice of buying votes before elections. Ludington remembered a riding organizer being called into Duplessis's office and being asked point-blank by the chief, "What does it take to win this riding?'' The man replied, ''These new-fangled washing machines are a wonderful thing. Maybe if I gave away washing machines to a number of prominent women in the community, they'd spread the word around, and their husbands would spread the word around, and this would get votes.''[15] The next day a ''number'' of washing machines were distributed in the riding.

King knew that in taking on Duplessis it was not simply a matter of issues (the Quebec government undermining the war effort), but that political combat would be entered into that included shady practices. While King was confident the odds were even in attacking Duplessis's imperious challenge of federal authority over the War Measures Act issue, he also instinctively recognized that to confront Duplessis on his own ground would be a bare-knuckles dust-up with no rule book.

Not surprisingly, King huddled with his own Quebec guard hours after the election was announced to begin planning his campaign strategy. He was indeed fortunate to be able to tap the resources of a remarkable trio of astute politicians: Ernest Lapointe, the federal minister of justice; Charles Gavan Power (affectionately known to everyone as ''Chubby''), recently appointed postmaster general; and P.J.A. Cardin, the minister of public works. Few prime ministers since have been lucky enough to have been served by such skilful operators as Lapointe, Power and Cardin, all now long dead, but who have become legends in the Liberals' Valhalla.

The undisputed leader was Lapointe, a towering bear of a man who served in three of King's ministries, twelve years as head of Justice. Born in St. Eloi, he attended Rimouski College, studied law at Laval University, and was called to the bar in 1898. Lapointe spoke not one word of English when he arrived in the House of Commons in 1904, representing Kamouraska. By 1939, Lapointe had not only become fluently bilingual, but was a masterful orator, confronting his audiences with a booming voice that shook with emotion and, when required, a talent for turning on a Niagara of tears for effect. In his early years in Parliament, Lapointe wore a huge belted overcoat and peaked cap, giving him the appearance of a calèche driver waiting with his horse outside of the Chateau Frontenac. Lapointe was an open book, a man of wit and substantial humour. Thérèse Casgrain, whose husband, Pierre, was secretary of state during the early years of the war, remembered one evening dining at Laurier House with King, the Lapointes and a visiting foreign dignitary, when King suddenly turned to the guest of honour and said, "You know, my dog can sing."[16] With this, King placed Pat on the piano stool, putting the dog's paws on the keys, and began to howl. Pat took up the refrain as the guests watched in discomfort. As they were driving home, Pierre Casgrain turned to Lapointe and asked the justice minister if he wouldn't mind talking to King about this embarrassing incident. Lapointe paused, nodded and said, "Yes. I think there is only one way. We'll have to speak to the dog."

King held Lapointe in deep respect, even in awe, not just because of his obvious parliamentary skills but because of his political virtuosity in the rough-and-tumble politics of Quebec. It was the one province King viewed with suspicion, whose church's influence he dreaded and whose language he never understood. Lapointe was to King what Cartier was to Macdonald, Fielding to Laurier. There was a deep bond between them.

Equally influential in Quebec was Chubby Power from Sillery, who presented a strange mixture of ingredients for a Quebec politician. Irish, Catholic and English-speaking, Power, like Lapointe, only learned his adopted tongue in his early twenties, but mastered the habitant's patois with ease and spoke it with a charming cadence. Before the androgynous age of the 1970s, Power would have been called a man's man. He smoked, was a prodigious drinker and a confirmed poker player. In his youth, he was a superb athlete who turned down a possible career in the NHL; instead he studied law at Laval. Power was a decorated World War I infantry officer who was so grievously wounded by a German rifle grenade in 1916 that he spent an entire year hospitalized in England. Speaking of his war service he said, "My war experiences were much the same as many another young man's: too much casual attention to training, binges in London, extravagant spending, all night sessions. Life in the trenches was a relief from the round of wild parties."[17] Power's drinking worried King. Six days before Duplessis called the provincial election, King considered appointing Power minister of national defence, but changed his mind fearing "he might break out at a critical time."[18] Presumably that meant going off on a terrible binge under pressure. As it turned out, Power was later given the post of minister of national defence, air, a post he distinguished himself in, serving with the same courage he displayed in the trenches of France.

At the moment, however, Power was more valuable to King as a grass-roots politician—a career that began before he entered his teens, as a campaign worker for his father, a federal member of Parliament. Power knew the elements required to succeed in Quebec politics: promises, pay-offs, patronage and a very large bankroll. At his own riding nomination meeting in 1917, he became the official Liberal candidate for Quebec South. But this was only after help from Jimmy O'Neil, his friend and a tavern-keeper from Quebec City's lower town. When it appeared as if Power was going to lose the nomination, O'Neil jumped up and yelled, "If Chubby Power does not emerge from this meeting as the official candidate, blood will be shed!"[19] He won and became a popular member of Parliament, loved by his constituents. His popularity was certainly further enhanced by his Irish good looks; with his smiling eyes, dashing moustache and expansive grin, Power looked like a handsome Mexican bandit.

The third member of King's Quebec triumvirate was P.J.A. Cardin. Somewhat less colourful than either Lapointe or Power, Cardin was a skilled parliamentarian and an effective platform speaker with an incisive mind. His only liability was a rather petulant suspicion of Anglo-Canadians, hardly a problem in these circumstances since he would not be campaigning in Moose Jaw but rather in Montreal or thereabouts.

A fourth and less visible figure was Raoul Dandurand, leader in the Senate. A patrician man with dazzling white hair, winged collars and proper length shirt cuffs, Dandurand appeared for all the world like some continental banker: reassuring, urbane and intelligent. He added sophistication to the upcoming operation; he was a man for whom King "had affection almost approaching veneration."[20]

King and his Quebec guard lost no time formulating strategy in the campaign against Duplessis. But what the guard proposed shocked

King. They'd pledge to resign from the federal Cabinet if Duplessis were re-elected, leaving no one from Quebec to protect the interests of French Canadians in Ottawa. It was a brilliant form of political blackmail, a risky gamble. In effect, Lapointe, Power and Cardin, all of whom were already on the public record opposing overseas conscription, were saying to Quebecers that if they chose Duplessis over them, there would be no one to oppose conscription by representing them in the inner circle of the Canadian government. Defeat Duplessis and win a guarantee that there would be no conscription. King at first was aghast, urging them not to be so candid. The three ministers said no, for without the promise of resignation, their case would be terribly weakened. In the end, King was persuaded. Conrad Black said the threat of Lapointe, Power and Cardin "was perhaps Canadian history's greatest turning of the political tables."[21] It may well have been.

Like knights off to the Crusades, the three Cabinet ministers and the aged senator quickly moved into the infidel Duplessis's home territory, dividing up the province into separate but key battle fronts. Power, besides serving as chief bagman, took over the Quebec City area; Cardin focused on Montreal; and the hulking Lapointe, like some lone ranger, went everywhere. Dandurand would work the Wedgwood set amidst the potted palms of Quebec's exclusive clubs, executive suites and respected hostelries.

The election campaign must qualify as the strangest ever in Canadian politics. Three federal Cabinet ministers and the leader of the Senate were actively, openly stumping the hustings although none was running for office. Chubby Power openly and brazenly dispensed federal largesse in a provincial election; and most bizarre of all, no one was paying much attention to the official provincial Liberal leader, Adélard Godbout, who, if they pulled off the operation, would be the next premier of Quebec.

From the beginning the campaign went badly for Duplessis. He refused to speak on radio because, with Canada at war, federal authorities demanded speeches in advance to check their contents to assure that remarks said in the heat of political battle would not serve the enemy. While Godbout launched his campaign within five days of the election call, Duplessis waited ten days. When he fired his opening fusillade in the courtyard of the Trois-Rivières Seminary, it was disastrous. Duplessis showed up drunk on a lethal mixture of gin and champagne. While he managed to stand erect and his words were not slurred, they made no sense. No one knew what he was talking about. This was not the case with Lapointe, who criss-crossed Quebec attacking Duplessis (he began calling Union Nationale the Union NAZInale) and pleading with Quebecers that they and only they could save the day.

"It heard from Lapointe a passion of oratory which Laurier had never excelled," wrote Hutchison. "It saw a towering black figure whose soul was poured nakedly into his pleading, whose outstretched arms seemed to embrace the province and the nation, whose face was knotted in pain and whose eyes often gushed tears."[22] The Pagliacci of politics, Lapointe's performance was Olympian.

Power, meanwhile, concentrated on keeping the war chest topped up, beginning with a loan from Saskatchewan Liberals. Midway through the campaign, when it began to look favourable for the Liberals, other contributions, as Power called them, began dribbling in. Money came from "persons who might be more naturally inclined to contribute to the government side but who, feeling that there was at least a chance of the provincial Liberals arriving in power, prudently thought to assure themselves of being well received by a potential new government."[23] There's no way of knowing how much money was spent. Power claimed it was less than the normal amount spent in provincial elections in Quebec, which isn't much by comparison. The money, according to Power, went to finance the candidates' campaigns and to "their financial representatives."[24] Power ran the money operation from his Quebec City law office through Isabel Gough, his private secretary. All transactions were, of course, in cash. When a pay-off was needed, Power sent a note by runner from his official campaign headquarters a few blocks away to Gough who, often carrying $50,000 in her purse, made personal deliveries. Amazingly, Gough carried these huge sums of money while travelling on trams and buses, taking her purse home at night without any protection. Said Power: "Perhaps because all this was done so openly and casually our opponents did not notice anything of a peculiar nature. I believe we were lucky during the election, and that we would have been wise to take precautions."[25]

The man with the most at stake, Mackenzie King, remained detached from the whole thing, receiving occasional progress reports, which indicated half-way through the campaign that victory was possible. On election night, King was driven to Ottawa's Experimental Farm, where he strolled alone for an hour before returning to Laurier House to monitor the official results on radio. Five minutes after the polls closed, there was no doubt that Lapointe, Power, Cardin and Dandurand had master-minded an incredible victory. When the last ballots were counted, the Liberals held seventy seats, to fourteen for the Union Nationale. While Maurice Duplessis was re-elected, his party was smashed, the end, as it was noted, to a "wildly hilarious government, largely carried on in hotel suites amidst numerous scandals, martinis, attendant ladies and bright red herrings."[26]

Naturally, King was enormously relieved, pouring out praise in his diary and signalling Lapointe's place in history "as far in esteem as that of Sir Wilfrid in the best of his days."[27]

The conquering heroes returned to Ottawa, Cardin by car, Lapointe and Power by train the following morning, arriving at Ottawa's Union Station where King was on hand to greet them in a wind-whipped rainstorm.

Lapointe appeared "tremendously pleased and relieved and happy," noted King.[28] Power, too, was exuberant under a cloud of alcohol even though it was only 11:30 A.M., a fact King recorded with peevishness. By 3:00 P.M., when King assembled his Cabinet, Power was completely drunk. He buttonholed King before the meeting with a demand that pay-offs be immediately rendered to several key party organizers whose efforts had helped bring victory. Power was adamant that Sir Eugène Fiset, the Liberal member for Rimouski, be made Quebec's lieutenant-governor "or some other appointment,"[29] for his work in the incredible campaign. King humoured Power the best he could even though Power was querulously drunk. King said the matter of Fiset's reward would be considered in due course. At this point Power threatened to resign, stomping out of Cabinet. King did call Fiset who, besides being a member of Parliament, was a retired major-general and veteran of the

Boer War. Fiset, a colourful old warrior, replied he was in no hurry and that he would consider any pay-off offer as long as it didn't affect his pension. Besides, he told King, he'd talk it over with Lapointe since both of them were leaving for a much-needed vacation. Power apparently went on a bender for two days.

These in-house Liberal squabbles, however, paled in the face of the results of the October 25, 1939, Quebec election. The exaggerated wish for victory had come true. "It is a great victory for the Allied cause," King mused. "Had the results gone the other way, Germany would have felt dismemberment of the British Empire had already commenced."[30] Hutchison said in 1952, "In retrospect it may be considered the most important election in modern Canadian history."[31] More important, perhaps, was the innate wisdom French Canadians displayed at a crucial moment of their history. Quebecers, continually called on to assess emerging political messiahs, invariably show impeccable judgement when it comes to endorsing or rejecting these saviours, and always at precisely the right moment. This they did in dispatching Duplessis. As events unfolded, it was not altogether a perfect solution, but one that at least bought time. It is also a nice historical question whether all the bag money and other "incentives" dispensed during that gloomy October were necessary. In this instance, it was the habitants' instincts that saved Mackenzie King, as much as the greasing of the palm and the monsoon of campaign booze.

Duplessis departed with a sober warning: "We shall have conscription in Quebec; I will be back, and next time I will stay for fifteen years. In the meantime they won't forget me."[32] All these prophesies would come true. The fiery promise by Lapointe, Power and Cardin that there would be no conscription would come to haunt them, all save the gallant Lapointe, who in two years would be dead, a victim of fatigue from too many campaigns.

Four months after the election, Adélard Godbout's first legislative session as Quebec premier opened on February 20, 1940. The Speech from the Throne was read by Sir Eugène Fiset who, as the newly appointed lieutenant-governor, was the picture of aloofness; he was a man who appeared to have risen above partisan politics.

CHAPTER TWO

Treason in Ontario

ANADA'S FIRST WARTIME CHRISTMAS was a sober one. In Ottawa, there were fewer coloured lights than the year before and less frivolity at the various government departments' Yuletide parties. But in the working-class neighbourhoods of Lower Town and LeBreton Flats, there was a picture-book quality to life that Christmas morning as smoke curled from kitchen wood stoves, mixing with a gentle falling snow.

From his windows in the library at Laurier House, King studied the surrounding landscape, listening to a lone church bell softly clanging out the hymn, *O Come All Ye Faithful*. Downstairs, servants had gathered around the radio to listen to George VI's annual Christmas morning message, a broadcast that left all in tears. When the prime minister joined them, he led the housemaids and kitchen help in singing *God Save the King*. King spent the rest of the day reading and answering the telephone calls from well wishers. At one point, a group of Salvation Army carolers appeared. Later in the evening, Joan and Godfroy Patteson arrived for a dinner of pheasant and partridge from the Experimental Farm, oysters from the Maritimes and a plum pudding. Served amidst table decorations of holly and chrysanthemums, King noted it as "a delicious Christmas repast."[1]

The prime minister deserved those few pleasant hours. He had earned the brief break. The first four months of war had been hectic and stressful, but productive. Since September, King had busied himself with a myriad of decisions, including new and important Cabinet appointments. J.L. Ralston, who retired from politics in 1935 to practise law in Montreal, had answered King's call to take over the Finance portfolio, replacing an ailing Charles Dunning. Norman Rogers was given Defence, taking responsibility away from Ian Mackenzie, someone King felt wasn't up to the task. There had also been the setting up of various Cabinet committees to streamline decision making. King intuitively knew this was going to be required in the business of running a war, the most important being the Emergency Council, which later became known as the War Committee of the Cabinet. King also kept close tabs on the formation of the First Division of the Canadian Army. The all-volunteer Expeditionary Force, led by General A.G.L. McNaughton, had already landed in Britain. Although no one knew at the time, many of the troops would not see Canada for another six years, inspiring some wags later to equate themselves with the Roman Legion for longevity of overseas service. The names of Ralston and McNaughton would dominate events yet to unfold. Of course no one had any inkling of the turbulent days ahead or the decisive roles each would play.

By the middle of December, King was extremely fatigued, partly brought on by his almost single-handed role in negotiating an agreement with London establishing the British Commonwealth Air Training Plan.

Perhaps the single most important contribution Canada was to make to the Allied cause, the role of this incredibly complex scheme was to become crucial as the air war reached its crescendo. King superstitiously orchestrated it so that it was signed on December 17, his birthday. Interestingly too, the agreement was viewed by King as spiritually motivated, one that would serve "the cause of Christianity itself against the forces of Paganism that were seeking to destroy Christian civilization."[2]

The stress of the Quebec election in October must have taken its toll of his energy as well. Even though King's part was passive, it was no less impressive. From the very beginning of the war, he displayed the capacity to actively seek and accept advice, however cautiously, as in the case of the Duplessis attack. His confidence none the less was admirable, confirming J.L. Granatstein's conviction that King "had few qualms about his ability as prime minister."[3] King had an assured sense of management that was apparent from the opening barrage of World War II.

As the last seconds of the old year slipped away, Mackenzie King, with little Pat at his side, faced 1940 through the window of his study, fearful in his thoughts about "what the New Year would bring," but conscious "of the Unseen Power" that was guiding him into the new year.[4] Outside, a cold, wind-driven rain had turned hard as steel on the roof-tops around Laurier House, and tree branches rattled like crystal in the moonlight below his bedroom window.

A pressing decision faced King in the opening days of 1940. His government's mandate was running out, and he would soon have to go to the people. In his favour was a period of twilight that had descended on most of Europe in the wake of the invasion of Poland. While the German army's Polish campaign had been wrapped up by October, the refitting of the army to man the Western Front against France was taking longer than the generals had anticipated. Western journalists, reduced to covering the war from the pubs of London and the bistros of Paris, grumbled over their drinks and peevishly dubbed the stalemate as the Phoney War, the Sitztkreig. The only shooting going on was in Finland where the Soviets had attacked at the end of November. King welcomed the stalemate. It would give him time to reach a decision about when to call an election. The last thing the prime minister wanted were raging battles and Canadian casualties while voters were going to the polls. The sooner he got the election over, the better. But when?

Early in 1940, King was handed an issue on a silver platter, and

unexpectedly from a strange quarter. Mitchell Hepburn, the premier
of Ontario and himself a Liberal, rose in the Ontario Legislature and
denounced Mackenzie King's wartime leadership. All members on
both sides of the House were momentarily stunned. Was "Mitch"
drunk again, many wondered. He often was. Neil McKenty, Hepburn's
biographer, wrote that there was nothing to indicate that Thursday,
January 18, would be an historic day at Queen's Park. George Drew,
the Conservative Opposition leader, was attacking Ottawa for not doing
more for the war effort. He urged the Ontario Legislature to "sound
a clear trumpet call to action,"[5] a familiar lament. Besides, almost
everyone regarded his remarks as purely partisan. But suddenly, Hepburn leaped to his feet, informing the members that he wanted to "be
associated with Colonel Drew in that attack on the King government."
He went further: "Let me say again that I stand firm in my statements
that Mr. King has not done his duty to his country — never has and
never will. I sat with him in the Federal House for eight years and
I know him." Hepburn's remarks reverberated around the chamber
like cannon fire. Then, reaching down to his desk, he pulled off a
piece of yellow paper from a doodling pad on which he had been
scribbling for the past few minutes. In a clear, strong voice he proposed
a resolution "regretting that the Federal government at Ottawa has
made so little effort to prosecute Canada's duty in the war in the
vigorous manner the people of Canada desire to see." A formal vote
was hurriedly recorded, although many Liberals ducked to their offices,
refusing to answer the Speaker's summons. But the damage was done,
forty-four to ten in favour of what became the Ontario War Resolution
condemning Mackenzie King's wartime leadership.

It was an extraordinary moment in the career of Mitch Hepburn.
One of the most astonishing politicians in Canadian history, he was
a reckless, ambitious and self-destructive figure whose own meteoric
rise to power during the Depression was the stuff of legends. There'd
never been anyone like Hepburn on any political stage in Canada, and
nothing matching the hateful feud between him and King. Years later,
Jack Pickersgill remarked that he didn't think King "was ever sure
why Mr. Hepburn had such aggrievements."[6] In fact, their animosity
was immediate from the moment they first met. Whatever can be said

against King, a vulgarian he never was; in fact, the opposite is true. A man of Victorian manners and social graces, King's feeling of repugnance toward Hepburn was entirely understandable. Hepburn was "flamboyant, boisterous, and a heavy drinker, all the things Mr. King most detested," remembered Pickersgill.

King's tormentor came from humble beginnings. Mitch Hepburn was born August 5, 1895, in southwestern Ontario's Elgin County, a farming Eden of rich black soil along the shores of Lake Erie. Hepburn grew up in St. Thomas and lived briefly in Winnipeg. A high-school drop out, a youthful bank clerk and farmer, Hepburn first ran as the Liberal candidate for Elgin West, winning a federal seat in the 1926 general election. He clashed with King immediately upon arriving in the House of Commons when he was assigned a distant back-bencher's seat (almost in the lobby, as he described it). King soothed the new member only to be further annoyed when Hepburn took on the Sun Life Assurance Company, criticizing a private bill that would increase Sun Life's capitalized stock. This was an attack that struck close to home since the old grey fox himself, Senator Dandurand, sat on the company's board of directors.

Hepburn's stock rose slightly in King's estimation following the 1930 federal election when R.B. Bennett, whose campaign pledge to blast Canada into the world markets, blasted the Liberals from power. Hepburn, however, was re-elected in Elgin West. King moved him into the front benches where he delighted in Opposition by taking on Bennett, the bombastic tycoon.

At the same time, Hepburn attracted the attention of the back-room boys in the Ontario Liberal Party. They'd been casting around for a prophet to lead the party out of the political wilderness where they had been wandering for a quarter of a century. King was reserved when they selected Hepburn to lead their renewed charge in Ontario, admitting Hepburn possessed ability but in his opinion "not of the cool, calculating kind."[7] Hepburn led the Liberals to a sweeping victory in 1934, taking sixty-six seats to the Tories' seventeen. At age thirty-seven, Hepburn became the youngest political leader in the history of Ontario. He was a man whose "friendliness and folksiness, his dynamism, his belligerency and even his personal excesses differentiated him from previous leaders."[8] As Ontario electors soon discovered, this was an understatement.

Hepburn's popularity was immense. He could do no wrong. He rejected the title of premier and began calling himself the prime minister of Ontario. Shortly after taking office, Hepburn carried through many of his campaign promises to pare provincial spending. He held a public auction in Varsity Stadium, selling off forty-seven government limousines. He fired hundreds of civil servants and political hacks the previous administration had appointed to various commissions and boards. The strangest blood-letting involved 183 provincial bee-keepers, whose political crimes were never stated. Predictably, the press likened Hepburn to Huey Long, the flamboyant governor of Louisiana, and compared the dismissal of civil servants to the beheadings that occurred during the French Revolution. Hepburn launched a series of official investigations into nearly every publicly administered provincial body, from the workings of the Temiskaming and Northern Ontario Railway to the personal files of the Commissioner of the Ontario Securities Commission, who just happened to be Colonel George Drew. Arthur Meighen, the former and short-lived Canadian prime minister, also was investigated for his dealings with the Ontario Power Service Corporation. Meighen fumed it was "the most diabolical political inquisition ever held outside Turkey, the conduct of it would put to shame Pontius Pilate."[9]

Hepburn's influence increased, or he thought it had, following his indefatigable campaigning in the 1935 general election on behalf of Mackenzie King's federal Liberals, whose return to power Hepburn believed was achieved in no small part by his appearance on the hustings. When Hepburn suggested to King that several cabinet appointments were in order for a couple of his friends as payment, he was rebuked by King for trying to interfere in federal politics. It was an upbraiding Hepburn would not soon forget.

In today's parlance, Hepburn was a swinger who, like Duplessis, also ran his government from hotel rooms; in Hepburn's case, it was a suite in Toronto's King Edward Hotel. There, on one occasion, Anthony Jenkinson, a British author, reported on Hepburn's style of executive management:

He wore a well-tailored, double-breasted suit and had the appearance and manner of a popular young man-about-town. From the room behind him came the sounds of radio dance music and ice tinkling in glasses and girls' voices. . . .

Mitchell Hepburn led me into the room where the radio was playing, and introduced me to his friends. They were his doctor and a member of his Government and two attractive girls who sprawled on the sofa and called the Prime Minister "Chief". . . . A big broad-shouldered fellow with the supple movements of a trained athlete mixed drinks and . . . periodically dashed out of the apartment after slipping on a camel-hair coat and light felt hat with the brim turned up in front. . . . It was evident that he acted as a sort of bodyguard-cum-gentleman's servant to the Prime Minister. The latter called him "Eddie," but the girls just called him "Bruiser."[10]

Hepburn dressed like a mobster in two-tone brogues, flannel suits with broad pinstripes in winter, and linen suits with white shoes in summer. There was a slight air of the cherub in his face, dominated by a dimpled chin under mischievous eyes. After drinking, his face took on the appearance of a candied apple on which someone had drawn one of those "have-a-nice-day" smiles. His drinking disgusted King, who frequently mentioned Hepburn's dissipated and hung-over appearance in the morning, especially during the royal visit of 1939.

Always restless and agitated, Hepburn was forever taking off for trips to the flesh pots of New York, Havana and Miami. His inner circle of friends was eclectic: There was Gene Tunney, the heavyweight boxing champion; "Sell em" Ben Smith, the New York financier; and J.P. Bickell, remembered as the Bay Street cowboy and mining magnate. Others included Harry McLean, the Canadian construction czar who built the Holland tunnel from Jersey to Manhattan; Frank O'Connor, of Laura Secord chocolate fame; L.J. "Larry" McGuinness, Toronto distiller; and of all people, Maurice Duplessis, whose friendship was often referred to by the press as "the unholy alliance." Duplessis and Hepburn shared much in common, not least of all a growing impatience in dealing with Mackenzie King over hydro power policy, timber rights, newsprint prices and taxation.

It seems remarkable that Hepburn carried on in this hedonistic

manner throughout the Depression when most people could barely
make ends meet. But he did, and in a style predating television's
Dynasty. When Hepburn wasn't in residence at the King Edward, or
on a drinking spree below the border, he and his friends gathered at
Hepburn's baronial homestead in Elgin County. Hepburn had inherited
much of the sprawling and productive 1200 acres of farmland he called
"Bannockburn Farms," with its wonderfully rambling white-brick
mansion. Entertaining was lavish, but a burden on Eva, his attractive
and apparently uncomplaining wife. It was a working farm whose main
crop was onions, yet the grounds featured a baseball diamond and
artificial swimming hole Hepburn called Lake Laurier. The house was
approached by a huge circular drive whose inner hub held carefully
tended ornamental trees and a profusion of flower beds beside which
his friends parked their limousines. It would have seemed Mitch
Hepburn had everything: power, prestige, a measure of wealth, a
courageous wife and three attractive children. Inexplicably, these were
not enough. His compulsive search for female companionship was
embarrassingly public and crude. Among those he coveted was the
wife of Alex Hume. He frequently asked the journalist, "Is your wife
still living with you?"[11] The question became so repetitive and annoy-
ing that one day Hume lashed back at the premier, "Mitch, you should
be horse-whipped in the public square the way you've treated Eva
with liquor and women. I don't want you ever to ask me if my wife
is still living with me." Having said that, Hume "squared off" with
Hepburn, ready to poke him one. Momentarily startled, Hepburn threw
back his head and laughed, saying, "Alex, you're absolutely right."
Hepburn never again inquired of Mrs. Hume's marital status.

All the same, Hepburn's carousals seemed not to diminish his popularity; rather, in some circles they were jokingly heralded, such as
the time the premier led a delegation of his cronies to New York to
be inducted into the Saints and Sinners Club, a fraternal society linked
to the Shriners. A club bulletin remembered the occasion as the case
of the "well-Primed Minister whose party acted as if each drink were
their last."[12]

Mackenzie King's first reaction when he heard the news of Hepburn's outburst was that Hepburn had been drinking. His second

response was a chilling denunciation of Hepburn and his "shocking betrayal of Liberalism and of Liberal principles."[13] It appeared to King an almost religious attack on his Liberal temple, as bad as some drunken ex-priest denouncing the Holy See. King judged the situation as "the most important night since the war began," one that clearly jeopardized the future of the government. There is no doubt King regarded Hepburn with contempt and disgust and as a minor figure. But minor figure or not, Hepburn had double-crossed him one too many times. This disloyalty could no longer be tolerated. For a man who usually moved with the speed of a snail, King's behaviour in dealing with Hepburn, as revealed in his diary, shows a crispness of thought uncharacteristic of his personality. He appears decisive and analytical. His first reaction expressed to Lapointe "was a general election at once." From that immediate reaction, King went on to build in his own mind a convincing case that he could safely call an election and win it. The most minute details did not escape examination, from the effect of a spring thaw on the attendance at the polls in the back concessions of the nation; to the logistics required of the chief electoral officer in getting the balloting machinery in place; to whether authority existed to record the soldiers' vote. (It didn't, but was made possible by provisions under the ever convenient War Measures Act.) Even a date was examined — March 26. While he consulted some members of his Cabinet and staff, the decision was solely his, confirming what Granatstein has said of King's judgement, "While not infallible, [he] was usually correct."[14]

On January 25, 1940, the day Parliament was to resume, King rose early and completed his morning Bible reading. When a vision of a star suddenly appeared in his thoughts, a vision that he felt was not without significance, the die was cast. Canadians, and for that matter most members of Parliament, learned in the Speech from the Throne of an immediate election, an announcement King gleefully recorded as being "certainly a real surprise to all who were present."[15] An even bigger surprise was a reference to dissolution of Parliament. Chubby Power had said there "was some doubt about the fairness"[16] of such a move, but King would hear no such talk. Referring to a recent speech by George Drew "that King must go,"[17] the prime minister told the

House of Commons "he was quite prepared to accept that slogan and go to the people."

Immediately after the House adjourned at six, the Cabinet met and adopted an order-in-council recommending dissolution. King himself took the document to Government House where it was signed at seven minutes past seven (again, the hands of the clock). The sixth session of the Eighteenth Parliament was over. Members who had gone out to eat found to their horror, when they returned to Parliament, that the doors of the House were closed. King had moved with the timing of a jockey, effectively cutting off any possible debate in Parliament or Opposition criticism of the government's war effort. Of course, it was all legal and constitutionally correct, but hardly a gesture one would expect from a sporting gentleman. King could hardly have forgotten that he had promised Robert Manion, the leader of the Tory opposition, when Parliament adjourned in September that there wouldn't be an election before dissolution.

And Manion was furious. A doctor from the Lakehead, Manion had been chosen with some expectation to succeed R.B. Bennett. Another convivial figure, Manion like Hepburn loved good company, good food and good drink. As a parliamentarian, however, he was handicapped by a laughable delivery, reminiscent of an auctioneer. Manion spoke so rapidly that Hansard reporters experienced considerable difficulty keeping up with his Gatling-gun cadence of speech. Manion's greatest liability, however, was underestimating King. After becoming Tory leader, Manion had been invited by King to tea at Kingsmere, a visit that included a tour of the strange ruins that King had constructed on the grounds of his country estate. Later, Manion told Richard Bell, who was private secretary to both R.J. Manion and R.B. Hanson, and later minister of citizenship and immigration in Diefenbaker's 1962 cabinet, he felt King "had taken leave of his senses,"[18] and decided that if he couldn't defeat King, "I don't deserve to be anything." On that wintry January day, King had spiked Manion's Gatling gun in full public view. Besides, in King's mind the idea that Manion was prime ministerial timber was a grotesque one. Now, he could turn his attention to Mitchell Hepburn and that other despicable Tory, George Drew; his election strategy would require the wisdom of Solomon.

Barely three months before, the Liberals had convincingly persuaded Quebecers that their future would be safeguarded in a world conflict, that no Québécois were going to be sent to fight and die in foreign lands. Yet, King now faced this new demand from Ontario Liberals and Conservatives alike for Ottawa to accelerate its war efforts. It would not be easy to finesse the disparity of the two positions. This was potentially perilous as it was no longer possible to avoid showing exactly where King stood.

For such a fence-sitter as King, this indeed would be a tremendous challenge. He met it with typical astuteness. King sensed that English Canada's mood would support a plea for national unity in facing the enemy, following a strong and forceful leadership. This only confirmed the opinion of H.H. Stevens, a long-time foe in the House of Commons, of King's keen perception ''to gauge public opinion''[19] and his flawless timing in knowing when ''to step out and wave the flag.''

While King took the high road during the campaign, Hepburn played dirty pool. He banned a showing in Ontario of an edition of *The March of Time* that featured Mackenzie King, labelling the film ''nothing but political propaganda of the most blatant kind.''[20] The manoeuvre backfired when Louis de Rochemont, the producer, cried foul, saying ''that this was the second time a *March of Time* film had been banned, the first time having been by Hitler.''[21] Ottawans got to see the film anyway, across the river in Hull.

The Liberal campaign was given a further boost when Manion called for the formation of a National Government, composed of members of all parties. King, who was usually ineffective on radio, surprised everyone in this campaign when he used the medium with unaccustomed skill, especially in the third of his national broadcasts on February 24 when he refuted Manion's plea for national government. It is worth quoting for the clarity and logic King presented to Canadians sitting impassively in front of their radios coast to coast:

> This war demands Canada's utmost effort. Such an effort can be made only by a government which draws its strength from every section of the country and has been given an unquestioned mandate by the people. Can you name any political group or combination

of men, other than the present government, which is likely to enjoy your confidence, or has the remotest chance of being representative of Canadian opinion as a whole? This is the vital question which you, the electors, must continue to ask yourselves between now and the 26th of March. If, in the interval, you have failed to take all these matters into account, it will be too late to retrace your steps once that day has passed.[22]

Hardly a barn-burner of a speech, but words that Canadians could easily follow. Most importantly, it was a speech that left a question to be answered by listeners—an old technique, yet effective. The King campaign was further aided by dissension in Hepburn's ranks. Halfway through the campaign, Hepburn's seat-mate in the Legislature, Harry Nixon, resigned from the Hepburn Cabinet as provincial secretary. It was a body blow from which Hepburn and his dissident Ontario Liberals never fully recovered. When Nixon, a bit of a rustic character, and his wife agreed to appear with King on the platform at Massey Hall in Toronto on March 14, Hepburn's credibility was nearly completely eroded. King, with Lapointe at his side, was given thunderous ovations; it was a night full with the scent of victory.

On election day, March 26, the Liberals won an overwhelming majority, taking 184 seats out of a total of 245. "We really cleaned up in the province of Quebec," King noted with satisfaction.[23] The victory there surprised many pundits. In Fort William, Manion lost his seat, thereafter disappearing from the national scene and returning to his farm to raise horses.

In a little over five months, Mackenzie King had destroyed Maurice Duplessis, demolished Manion and discredited Hepburn to such an extent that Ontario's premier never fully recovered. This was not helped by King's final order in the campaign battle to Liberal back-room boys in Ontario that he "wanted Mitch to be ousted."[24] In due course Hepburn vanished from the scene, emotionally beaten, physically dazed from too much booze, and altogether disconsolate. But there was to be one more show-down with King.

Mackenzie King had won a ringing endorsement from the nation to carry on as Canada's wartime prime minister, leaving in his wake some of the most colourful flotsam in Canadian politics.

After the shoot-out, when the smoke had cleared, Bob Manion the Conservative wrote to Hepburn, the disgraced Liberal, thanking him for his help in this strange alliance that had failed to unseat Mackenzie King. His words were: "Just a note of appreciation for all you tried to do in our behalf—or at least against the fat little jelly fish out at Kingsmere, but somehow he seems to come out on top."[25]

King always did.

CHAPTER THREE

Foes and a Friend

ACKENZIE KING'S DESTRUCTION OF opponents was accomplished by extremely polished political skill. This certainly was not the case concerning ordinary foes, those faceless latrine lawyers sounding off in the washrooms of the war plants, or the ordinary citizen into his cup at the corner beer parlour. Seven days before Canada formally declared war, the staff of the Justice Department of Ottawa, citing provisions in the War Measures Act, produced sinister regulations on the Canadian democracy. This was the Defence of Canada Regulations, which virtually banned free speech and outlawed numerous ethnic social clubs suspected of undermining social order in wartime Canada. The legislation created an atmosphere that could only be described as comic hysteria. King, disturbed by mounting public criticism, eventually ordered a review of the regulations, but not before 1000 citizens were arrested by RCMP and local police departments.

Many of the cases bordered on the absurd. Take the example of a graduate of Tampa's Mystic Brotherhood University, the Rev. Rees, who suddenly found himself arrested, handcuffed, fingerprinted and thrown into a jail cell for what he called preaching the "love of Jesus."[1] Toronto police produced evidence of his subversion when they found this card in the window of his home: "Warriors are unwelcome—the church of Jesusitis, teaching the ancient occult lore of Yoga wisdom was, is and will be always at peace with man or beast. . . . Thus we declare 'war is anathema'." Rees was eventually acquitted. However, there was no acquittal for Gustaf Bolling, who was fined $25 and costs for greeting a soldier in a Kingston beer hall with "Heil Hitler," and saying, "Blast the British." A slightly hung-over Mr. Bolling pleaded guilty to the charges. In Montreal, police burned three tons of Communist literature including a copy of *Time* magazine with Trotsky's picture on it. In January 1940, King, hoping to cool emotions and to fend off his critics, convinced his colleagues in the Cabinet of "the desirability of having a committee of Parliament review the Defence Regulations."[2] He got immediate support from Chubby Power, who suggested that all orders-in-council be placed before a committee of the House for review. Years later, Power recalled that by the beginning of that year he had become "generally fed up with political events."[3] He strongly objected to some of the extraordinary measures being enacted under the WMA which he felt "weakened parliamentary institutions and government, and placed tremendous power in the hands of the police." Power wrote King a letter on January 4 informing him of his concern, but he never sent the letter. On January 18, however, King got agreement from his ministers to carry out a review, but noted that Lapointe feared that such a review could only increase and not lessen the trouble. The astute justice minister was correct in his thinking. Later amendments were even more severe. In the early months of the war, newspaper reports of those prosecuted under the Defence of Canada Regulations usually quoted the remarks made by the accused, which were considered to be an offence. The amendments did not allow the press to be specific so it became impossible for the public to learn the exact crimes of these vocal dissidents. For instance, Jan Scheper, a Montreal house painter, was sentenced to six months for making "disloyal remarks."[4] H.R. Hanson, a Great Lakes sailor from Toronto, had been arrested for "spreading false rumours." In each case the press was prevented from reporting what constituted disloyal remarks or false rumours. The numerous arrests, if they did nothing else, created alarm in the minds of Canadians. Concerned with reports of these anti-patriotic remarks, a custodian at Sir Henry Pellatt's farm in Toronto's King township announced that 1,100 Fenian raid muzzle-loaders had been removed from Sir Henry's estate and taken to the armories downtown for fear they would fall into the hands of fifth columnists.

Exactly how many suspects were arrested is impossible to say. The RCMP records show a total of 1,365 arrests were made from September 3, 1939, to March 31, 1941. How many others were arrested by local police departments is not known. The Italian community represented the largest number of those arrested. Police interned 558 Italians, including at least two who were arrested even before Italy had entered the war on June 10, 1940. The German-Canadian community saw 375 of their number hauled away by police. The most celebrated case, however, did not involve some drunken malcontent or Axis sympathizers but none other than Camillien Houde, the outlandish but very popular mayor of Montreal.

For many years, Camillien Houde had ruled the city as a benevolent dictator heading a régime that operated openly on the principle of graft. Houde had insisted that influential citizens pay for their favours, and his administration never looked on the practice of graft as other than a unique accounting system that fell into the category of payment for services rendered. He was often referred to as the Robin Hood of municipal affairs, accepting money from the well-to-do and giving it out to large groups of beggars who were constantly waiting in his anterooms. Houde was not below such shady practices as buying loyalty, either, especially from journalists. The city gave newspapermen covering city hall $1000 a year, paid quarterly. When Tracy Ludington first appeared as a young reporter to cover the city beat, he was told by the chairman of the city hall press gallery, "Oh, you've come the right day, tomorrow's pay-day."[5] Ludington, who worked for the *Gazette*, was under strict orders, however, not to accept any money. Still, the gallery chairman stuffed a cheque into his breast pocket, but Ludington return it by mail with a letter saying the cheque was inadvertently made out to him and he was returning it. A couple of months later, he was called before a member of Houde's executive committee and asked, "I understand that you don't take cheques?" When Ludington replied that was correct, he was informed that he could "have cash if you prefer."

Houde's style of governing was as unorthodox as his personality. A six-footer, Houde weighed more than 300 pounds. He was reputed to eat a box of chocolates a day between copious meals of Chinese food or huge bowls of spaghetti brought from surrounding restaurants by his valet-chauffeur. Houde was anything but attractive. With his oversized head he looked like a circus elephant man. His homeliness was only overshadowed by his eccentric dress. No one was shocked, for instance, if the mayor arrived at the office in the morning entirely in green: green suit, green shirt, green tie and green socks. While Houde's sartorial appearance clashed with Mackenzie King's staid style of dress, it was his fervent feeling of independence as a Quebecer that brought him into direct confrontation with the prime minister.

On June 22, 1940, Royal Assent was given to a bill the government had introduced in the House of Commons the previous day. It was the National Resources Mobilization Act requiring Canadians to place themselves and their property at the disposal of the King in any way deemed necessary for the defence of Canada. Said Stacey: "It thus authorized compulsory military service, but (in accordance with the Government's pledges) limited it to home defence."[6]

In a strange twist of fate, Tracy Ludington now found himself directly involved in Houde's opposition to King and Ottawa. After serving four years as a city hall reporter, Ludington in August 1940 was appointed as the city editor of the *Gazette*. On August 2, Ludington got a nervous call from the man who had replaced him at city hall. The reporter informed Ludington that Houde had just told a bunch of reporters in his office that he was going to advise Quebecers not to sign up for national registration. The reporter wanted to know how the story should be handled. Ludington told the reporter to type out a statement of Houde's remarks and have the mayor sign it. When the reporter suggested that Houde was not that foolish, Ludington replied, "Type it out, take it in and get him to sign it. I know the man very well. He's

too proud to let you think that he would back down. He'll sign it."[7]
Shortly after, the reporter was back in the *Gazette* offices with the
signed statement from the mayor urging all male Quebecers not to
answer the call to register. "It is unequivocally a measure of conscription," the statement said.[8] Houde reminded Montrealers specifically and Quebecers generally that both King and their newly elected
provincial leader, Premier Godbout, had publicly proclaimed there
would be no conscription under any circumstances. If the National
Resources Mobilization Act wasn't conscription, then what was?
Houde asked.

The story appeared in the *Gazette*'s first edition of August 3 but
was quickly pulled from later editions by the government censor who
believed the remarks were seditious. Ludington, not to be foiled by
the bureaucrats, telephoned R.B. Hanson, the newly elected leader of
the Conservative Opposition in Ottawa (he replaced Manion). Hanson
read the statement in the House of Commons and demanded to know
what the government intended to do in the face of this illegal challenge
to King's leadership. He need not have asked. Houde's future was as
predictable as the instructions in the game of Monopoly: go to jail.
King was more miffed at Hanson than Houde. "Hanson's questions
clearly were of a political nature," King wrote in his diary, "calculated
to make trouble between the government and the press, also to stir
up trouble in Quebec."[9] The warrant for Houde's arrest was signed
by Ernest Lapointe himself. As the flamboyant mayor was leaving city
hall on the evening of August 5, he was charged under the Defence
of Canada Regulations.

To King's immense relief, there was no backlash from Quebecers
over Houde's arrest, or his subsequent internment for the rest of the
war. Houde, in all his bulk, was transported to Camp Petawawa in
Ontario where he served his time as Canada's most famous political
prisoner. Equally surprising was Houde's attitude toward Tracy
Ludington, the man who was instrumental in having him locked up.
Like all good politicians, Houde always remembered the birth dates
of his more notable constituents and acquaintances. Every year of the
four Houde was behind bars, he never forgot to send Ludington a
birthday card and gift. Ludington never thought this gesture unusual.

"I think he realized that I had been instrumental in helping to make him a martyr in his own lifetime," said Ludington with a chuckle many years later.[10] When Houde was eventually released, he returned to Montreal where he was given a tumultuous welcome by a crowd of 10,000, being carried on the shoulders of an honour guard from the train station to his home. Re-elected as mayor, Camillien Houde was never defeated again. The Houde incident was just one of many that reflected Mackenzie King's paranoia when dealing with opposition, be it from small-fry malcontents in the beer parlours of the nation or the chambers of any elected government. He constantly fumed in private against all foes he suspected were undermining his leadership. It seemed he never had a real friend, if we believe his diary musings. But when he did strike up a friendship he felt was genuine, King became effusive with praise and recorded in detail all aspects of the relationship. Such was the case of his remarkably warm friendship with Franklin Delano Roosevelt, the president of the United States.

Everyone affectionately called him FDR, and he was one of the most popular men in American public life in this century. There was a quality of nobility about the man. Born to a wealthy and privileged family, he chose to serve in public life: as a senator for the state of New York, later as assistant under secretary of the Navy, and finally as the Democratic governor for New York. In 1921, when Franklin Delano Roosevelt was at the height of a distinguished career, he was suddenly struck down by poliomyelitis, turning him into a wheelchair cripple for the rest of his life. This handicap did not prevent him from successfully running for the presidency in 1932, winning 42 of the then 48 states of the union.

FDR exuded warmth, wit and unpretention, and although he was just as likely to be found on Vincent Astor's yacht, these aristocratic connections were never a liability with the American voter. Although the blue-blood, upper-crust layer of American republicanism viewed him as a traitor to the ideals of conservatism, his popularity was immense with the ordinary man. One Jewish couple was so pleased with his victory on election night, they recorded the name of their new-born son as Franklin Delano Finkelstein. If the business of America under the Hoover administration was American business, FDR's business was the business of reconstruction. His arrival at the White House came at the height of the Depression. To his conservative critics he soon began showing, in their opinion, his true colours as a left-wing liberal. Launching a series of startling measures to combat the economic slide, FDR soon had America moving again. He paid farmers not to farm; he took the U.S. off the gold standard, launched his Civilian Conservation Corps and put to work thousands of unemployed slum youths. Americans soon came to respect this forceful figure who dazzled them with grace, candour and swift action. All were attributes one could not apply to the leader of America's northern neighbour.

FDR and Mackenzie King had little in common. True, they both had gone to Harvard but hadn't met until long after graduation. Shortly after King regained power in 1935 he had arranged a visit to Washington. Lawrence Martin, in his *The Presidents and the Prime Ministers*, wrote, "The popularity of the president was not a fact that would escape Mackenzie King at this time or at any time during the thirteen-year stewardship of FDR."[11] Both leaders used one another throughout their tenures of office; King cashed in by merely being seen with FDR, who was as popular in Canada as he was at home, and Roosevelt bounced ideas off King, whose adroitness in political matters did not go unnoticed by the American president. Oddly enough, too, both men trusted one another. It was a successful relationship that was productive and genuine. Historian Donald Creighton said King was nothing more than a door mat at one of the two wartime Quebec Conferences; others claim King enjoyed the position of middle-man between Roosevelt and Churchill. Actually this was true in both cases but it did not detract from the real friendship the two men enjoyed.

Also, in the era of suspicion between Canada and the U.S. that followed World War II, the King-Roosevelt friendship was incredibly informal, if not downright casual. As the war clouds took rapid and discernible shape on the European horizon, Roosevelt publicly stated that Canada could certainly count on the U.S. in any show-down with a belligerent Hitler. Speaking at Queen's University in Kingston in 1938 he told his audience: "I give to you the assurance that the people of the United States will not idly stand by if domination of Canadian soil is threatened by any other empire."[12] This commitment was later ratified in a more formal document, but in informal surroundings at a meeting between King and FDR at Ogdensburg, New York, in mid-August 1940. It was nothing less than the establishment of a Canadian-U.S. permanent joint defence board, arrived at by the two men without any consultation with either of the government parties' respective cabinets.

The directness of King's and Roosevelt's dealings were evident from the very beginning of the war. Although Britain had declared war on September 3, 1939, Canada was still lingering over the decision in Ottawa. On September 5, the telephone rang in King's East Block office. On the line was the president.

"We are having a discussion here," he told King, "and you can settle it. Is Canada at war?"[13]

King replied that only Parliament could decide that.

"Well, you will be soon, won't you?" asked FDR.

When King said yes, a relieved Roosevelt turned for a moment to someone in his office and said, "You see, it's all right." Roosevelt was decidedly nervous, for under debate in Washington was whether the U.S. could send tools of war to Canada because of America's Neutrality Act. Britain's declaration of war made it impossible to receive the goods directly because the U.S. was pledged not to support an active belligerent. Since Canada was at the moment still neutral, Roosevelt felt relieved, as all kinds of planes, guns and munitions were already being hustled across the border into Canada.

There wasn't any question that King and FDR enjoyed a happy relationship throughout the war. Certainly in Roosevelt's view, King was someone whose discretion he could rely on, and for King there was immeasurable public relations as being seen as a confidant of the most powerful man on the earth. In any case, the two leaders came to trust each other and to rely on one another's advice and support. At the end of the first week of December 1941, that trust was cemented in blood. For the first time they faced together a common enemy: Japan.

PART II

THE WAR IS REAL
December 1941–
July 1942

CHAPTER FOUR

Death in the Orient

ONE OF THE GREATEST propaganda deceits of World War II was the image projected of the Japanese soldier by the Allies. He was depicted as a bandy-legged, buck-toothed, myopic figure, who stared down the sights of his antiquated rifle through glasses as thick as the bottom of Coke bottles, members of "a blinky-eyed, toothy Gilbert and Sullivan race."[1] Canadians and Americans were also led to believe the Japanese fighting man went into battle wearing a G-string and funny looking boots that had a special compartment for the big toe, which he used to advantage to swing from "tree to tree, like Tarzan."[2] In the field he subsisted on fish heads, rice and liberal amounts of the Oriental schnapps, sake. Like all propaganda, there were minor truths in the description. The Japanese soldier did indeed wear odd footwear, and he did carry rice rations into battle. What the propagandists didn't say was that the Japanese soldier's fighting rations lasted five days and he packed 400 rounds of ammunition, twice the amount of U.S. infantrymen. Further, soldiers of the Rising Sun were stubborn in defence, fighting to the death for their country and emperor. As U.S. Marines discovered, the only way to defeat this soldier was to annihilate him by bomb, bayonet or flame as he dug into his gopher hole for the last stand. On the offence, the Japanese soldier was fearless. "Never let the Jap attack you," Douglas MacArthur warned his Pacific commanders, which they frequently did in suicidal banzai charges.[3] "The Japanese may have been the most underrated infantry weapon in history," said William Manchester, the American writer-historian who fought the Japanese soldier from island to island across the Pacific battleground.[4] While G.I.s and Marines would bear the brunt of battle in the Pacific, it was the Canadian infantryman who first met the Japanese soldier in battle, the results of which were catastrophic and one of the sorriest episodes in Canadian military history. Fifty years later, the mere mention of the name Hong Kong still conjures up memories of terrible sacrifice, Canadian military ineptness and negligence.

Six hours after the Imperial Navy's devastating attack on Pearl Harbor in the Hawaiian Islands, the Japanese Army launched its assault on Hong Kong, wiping out in the first minutes of battle the tiny (only six planes) RAF air defence. The date was December 8, 1941. By Christmas Day, the Japanese had captured the British Crown colony, the first of many Pacific victories that at the height of the conflict had spread to encompass a tenth of the world's surface. How two Canadian infantry battalions came to be on the besieged island of Hong Kong was, with the disastrous landings of Canadians at Dieppe, one of the two great horror stories of World War II, reeking with evidence of poor judgement and monumental incompetence. It was an episode that Mackenzie King painfully described as the most distressing of any that faced his government, and one that contained the potential to destroy him and his government. That King survived the crisis was nothing short of a miracle and attested once more to his political skills.

In the eyes of some historians, the story is complicated and the facts sometimes vague and contestable. Not so in the case presented by Carl Vincent in his definitive examination, *No Reason Why*. It is a numbing indictment of all participants, political and military, who committed the Winnipeg Grenadiers and the Royal Rifles of Canada to the defence of Hong Kong, barely weeks before battle erupted. "The Canadians who fought at Hong Kong in December 1941 and either died in the hopeless struggle or else passed into a brutal and all too often fatal captivity are the possessors of a unique distinction,'' wrote Vincent. ''They are the only Canadian soldiers and possibly the only Commonwealth soldiers of the Second World War who were deliberately sent into a position where there was absolutely no hope of victory, evacuation, or relief.''[5]

The hopelessness of defending the Crown colony had long been recognized by any number of British Army defence planners; Winston Churchill, himself, decided against it as late as January 1941. ''If Japan goes to war with us,'' he wrote, ''there is not the slightest chance of holding Hong Kong or relieving it. It is most unwise to increase the loss we shall suffer there. Instead of increasing the garrison it ought to be reduced to a symbolical scale.''[6] Churchill's reaction came in the face of a proposal from one of his generals, A.E. Grasett.

Six months later, in the summer of 1941, Major General Grasett, who was Canadian born, passed through Ottawa, where he met his old friend Major General H.D.G. ''Harry'' Crerar, then Chief of the Canadian General Staff. Crerar and Grasett were contemporaries at Kingston's Royal Military College. (Grasett left Canada following graduation, joining the British Army where he spent his military career.) When Grasett met Crerar in Ottawa he had just left Hong Kong as the General Officer commanding the garrison there. But he took away with him a belief (Vincent said it had become an *idée fixe*) that Hong Kong could be defended in the event of war. Although we'll never know the answer for certain, it seems Grasett convinced Crerar that two additional battalions, if sent to Hong Kong, would make the difference in mounting a creditable defence of the Crown colony.

At any rate, Grasett, back in Britain by September 3, reported to the War Office and the Imperial Chiefs of Staffs proposing that the Hong Kong garrison be strengthened by two battalions and that ''Canada could probably find the troops.''[7] The proposal ended up on Churchill's desk September 10, endorsed by the Chief of the Imperial General Staff. Why Churchill had changed his mind from a previous recommendation by Grasett in January is not entirely clear. But he did, and accepted the recommendation. On September 19, 1941, the Canadian government was formally asked to supply two battalions to strengthen the four British battalions already there. The MOST SECRET telegram informed Canada that approved policy now dictated Hong Kong be defended as long as possible in the event of war. Besides, British planners noted, "there have been signs of a certain weakening in Japan's attitude towards us and the United States."[8]

The War Committee of the Cabinet discussed the request on September 23. King and others agreed in principle with the request, but not before asking the opinions of J.L. Ralston, the Minister of National Defence, and General McNaughton, still in England where he was promoted to Lieutenant-General to command the newly formed VII Corps. Ralston was reticent, but after being assured by Crerar "that the Canadian Army should take this on,"[9] the defence minister stamped his approval. McNaughton also concurred. On October 20, King and his war ministers committed two battalions to Hong Kong.

The soldiers who were eventually picked to join the British garrison in Hong Kong were themselves mediocre garrison troops in terms of fitness, training and quality of equipment. The Winnipeg Grenadiers had spent the last sixteen months in Jamaica, virtually all of that period doing guard duty. The troops had very little training, and their numbers were significantly reduced by a high rate of illness, mostly malaria and dengue fever.

The Royal Rifles of Canada hadn't fared much better since war began. They had spent the previous ten months in Newfoundland guarding airfields at Botwood and Gander before being posted to the St. John's area for coastal defence duties. Guard duties and bad weather in Newfoundland had prevented any serious training. The members of the Royal Rifles were drawn from Quebec City, the Eastern Townships, the Gaspé and New Brunswick.

The two battalions sailed from Vancouver on October 27, minus four men from the Royal Rifles who went over the hill at the last moment. As well, forty members of the Grenadiers failed to show up. On the eve of sailing there was a minor mutiny by about forty soldiers who, complaining about conditions below, jumped ship. However, they were persuaded to board before the *Awatea* slipped her moorings. The battalions were about six per cent under strength, and many of the new replacements who volunteered had only the most basic training.

Finally, 212 vehicles arrived after the *Awatea* left port, and while valiant attempts were made to get most of the battalions' lost vehicles to Hong Kong, they never reached the ill-fated outpost. Of the 1,975 men who set sail, 557 never saw Canada again.

Peacetime troop-ship passages are inevitably boring, as was life aboard *Awatea* and HMCS *Prince Robert*, the escort that carried about one hundred men of the Hong Kong expedition. Tedium was momentarily relieved when the ships stopped briefly in Honolulu, where authorities arranged a demonstration of hula dancers at dockside, upon whom the soldiers showered packets of cigarettes and money.

The ships were crowded and hot, and there were long lines into the messes where mealtimes were staggered in order to feed everyone. It was only when they were at sea that the Canadians were told of their destination. Half-hearted shipboard training attempts were carried out and the men got lectures about Hong Kong. One soldier, a diabetic, died during the voyage, and authorities discovered a stowaway. The force reached Hong Kong November 16. In three weeks' time the Canadians were fighting for their lives.

Before the war, garrison duty in the colony was surprisingly pleasant. Hong Kong offered many diversions. There were plenty of clubs and interesting sightseeing tours available and, being one of the wicked cities of the world, Hong Kong offered sexual entertainment to sailors and soldiers far from home. The Canadians settled into camp life with relative ease, surprised that Chinese servants were assigned to chores they themselves would normally have done, such as cleaning their billets and kitchen duty. The Canadian officers shortly gained a reputation as good dancers at the officers' messes.

The Canadians lost no time digging into defensive positions along the colony's ragged coastline, preparing to repel an attack from the sea. But on December 8 when the Japanese attacked, the assault came from the opposite direction through Kowloon, spearheaded by the 38th Division, which was supported by two additional artillery regiments, two anti-tank battalions, an engineering regiment and three transport regiments. This force was much superior to the 14,000 defenders whose total number included St. John Ambulance personnel, nurses and the Hong Kong Mule Corps. The myth that the sons of Nippon were bedraggled troops in ill-fitting uniforms and disadvantaged by poor eyesight was quickly dispelled. The 38th Division was tough, well-trained and had already had a year in the field in China. Within a week, the Japanese had overrun the mainland peninsula of Kowloon and the so-called New Territories, pushing the defenders back to Hong Kong Island itself.

By Christmas Day, the Japanese had surrounded various remnants of defenders scattered in last-ditch pockets of resistance. On December 25, the Canadians and British surrendered; some of the units were out of ammunition, supplies and water. C.P. Stacey, never exuberant in writing history, had this to say about Canada's first major land battle and the men of the Winnipeg Grenadiers and Royal Rifles: "They had no chance for the gradual acquisition of battle wisdom through experience. The extraordinarily rugged and largely unfamiliar terrain of Hong Kong was one of the hardest battlefields on which Canadians fought in any theatre; and after their long sea voyage, followed by brief training for a static role which was never realized, the Royal Rifles and Winnipeg Grenadiers were not in the best shape for fighting on scrub-covered mountainsides. These adverse circumstances inevitably reduced the units' tactical efficiency. How hard they fought in spite of such conditions, their casualty lists fully and poignantly show."[10] Carl Vincent also concluded that despite attack after attack and against overwhelming odds, the Canadians never broke but he asked, "Did the odds *have* to be so heavily stacked against them?"[11]

It was an urgent question that Canadians themselves soon began to ask, and one that Mackenzie King attempted to answer. When the new session of Parliament opened January 22, 1942, R.B. Hanson, who had taken over as the new leader of the Opposition from the hapless Manion, demanded that a full-scale inquiry into the débâcle at Hong Kong be conducted by a parliamentary committee. King had no choice but to agree to the suggestion. There was no doubt in King's mind that someone had bungled horrendously in recommending the Hong Kong expedition. He told his diary that night that such an inquiry would really be "a help to us as it will show where the onus really lies, how ready we were to meet a British request, and will put the blame where it ought to be, on those responsible for taking some men

overseas who should not have gone.''[12] But King soon had second
thoughts about a parliamentary inquiry and the likelihood for free-for-
all politicking that committee members would surely bring into such
an open debate. King privately asked Hanson and M.J. Coldwell, leader
of the C.C.F. Party, to accept a judicial inquiry instead. Surprisingly,
they agreed, buying King's argument that a judicial inquiry was better
because it was non-partisan.

Sir Lyman Duff, the Chief Justice of the Supreme Court, was
appointed as commissioner of the Royal Commission. The hearings,
which were *in camera*, lasted twenty-nine days, examined 300 exhibits
and heard from sixty witnesses. Duff's findings, released in early June
1942, laid no blame on anyone for the ill-fated expedition, except for
the officer who missed the boat with the shipment of vehicles. King
was ecstatic with the results, saying, ''Its wording really made me
rejoice,'' and adding gloatingly, ''Both the Tories and the C.C.F. will
get the surprise of their lives when I read the Hong Kong report tomorrow.''[13] However, Canadians at the time had benefit only of the findings, not of the testimony.

As Vincent's detailed study of the testimony has since revealed,
there was every reasonable doubt whether the battalions were really
fit for battle. They were under strength, replacements were not much
more than raw recruits, they lacked certain weapons and ammunition,
and the bulk of the soldiers lacked advanced training. The quality of
testimony given by members of the military establishment was deeply
suspect. General McNaughton, although he had no official role in
recommending the dispatch of the troops, appeared as an expert witness
and testified that he detected no incompetence involved in the selection
of the doomed battalions, or any suspicion of a lack of their efficiency.
No one, either, had specifically asked British authorities what suddenly
had caused a change in Japan's attitude toward the Allies.

Clearly Crerar, as the evidence showed, had bought Grasett's plan
and promoted it with little thought of the consequences. Besides, Crerar
himself dodged any suggestion of military culpability by shifting blame
to the politicians. In a deposition to the Royal Commission, Crerar
wrote, ''In the case of the despatch of Canadian troops to Hong Kong
. . . political and moral principles were involved rather than military

ones, and on such a basis, the matter required to be considered and decided by the War Committee of the Cabinet."[14] Vincent concluded the testimony was an evasion of responsibility that would undoubtedly have caused Pontius Pilate to send out for a second wash-basin.

Vincent's definitive research into the mess leaves no doubt whatsoever of incompetence, poor judgement, and most damning of all, a gross lack of military intelligence of the situation in the Far East, which was threateningly intense. Even King, according to Pickersgill, "had expected war with Japan all through 1941."[15] Why the Canadian military minds decided in the face of all these facts to send troops to Hong Kong remains a scandalous mystery.

Of the untenable position Sir Lyman found himself in, Vincent had this to say: "Duff, no matter how impartial, could hardly, in mid-1942, have called into question the entire management of the war. Even a mild censure of the government's role in the affair could have had very wide political repercussions. Duff would no doubt have been prepared if necessary to do this in the case of impropriety or illegal activities on the part of government members, but not in judging the management of the war effort. That was the duty of Parliament or, in the final analysis, the duty of the electorate."[16]

In assessing blame, Grasett has to take his full measure for his obsession with defending an indefensible position (which all had agreed was the case), and Harry Crerar for not doing his homework, as one would have expected from his lofty position as Chief of the Canadian General Staff. As for King and the War Committee of the Cabinet, there is no hint that he or any of its members acted in any way other than in the best interests of a nation at war. They acted on the advice of their experts which, in the last analysis, was terribly wrong, much the same kind of advice that the late President John Kennedy got from his experts in the invasion of the Bay of Pigs in Cuba. In either case, both participants, while it is debatable whether they could be held accountable, must share the responsibility.

More important than who was to blame for Hong Kong was the demonstration by King, at a crucial moment, of a rare ability that few commanders possess: the capacity to absorb defeat, involving painful loss of life, and to get on to the next battle of the war. Admittedly, this was of little solace to surviving members of the Hong King expedition or to their families, or for succeeding generations of Canadians since Hong Kong.

Even more unfathomable was the subsequent behaviour of the victorious Japanese soldier who, in the words of Stacey, showing a rare burst of emotion, "sullied his victory at Hong Kong by acts of barbarism worthy of savages."[17] The surviving Canadians suffered indescribable horrors at the hands of their captors: torture, starvation and murder, conduct so despicable that they defy understanding or forgiveness; acts apparently committed under the mystical Japanese code of conduct called Bushido which, among its many principles, calls for disdain of *noblesse oblige* towards inferiors, whom the Canadians became when they chose to surrender rather than die in battle.*

The defeat at Hong Kong was to have immediate repercussions at home, creating another crisis for Mackenzie King. Reaction to Hong Kong and the air attack on Pearl Harbor resulted in immediate and virulent attacks on Japanese Canadians living on the west coast. Although many of them were citizens and had led exemplary lives in the Canadian democracy, which they had come to love and trust, King and society soon branded them as outcasts.

---

*Ironically, Chubby Power's son, Francis, served as a lieutenant with the Royal Rifles in the Hong Kong siege. Wounded in action, Power, Jr., received the Military Cross for outstanding courage and leadership under fire. He survived captivity. Oddly, in Power's autobiography, *A Party Politician*, there is no reference to his son. The Quebec politician may also have informally suggested the Royal Rifles as one of the two units sent to Hong Kong. At the Royal Commission hearing, Power admitted he never questioned anyone about whether defence of the Colony was feasible.

CHAPTER FIVE

The Enemy that Never Was

THE JAPANESE ATTACK ON Pearl Harbor on December 7, 1941, was spectacular. In less than three hours, the carrier-borne raiders destroyed or damaged fourteen battleships, cruisers and destroyers, and wiped out nearly all of the American navy and army planes based in the Hawaiian Islands. As the Japanese torpedo-bomber and fighter pilots zoomed back to their waiting aircraft carriers off-shore, they left behind 2,400 dead Americans, and almost complete devastation at the sprawling U.S. naval base.

In retrospect, the attack was a colossal strategic and tactical mistake. Instead of demoralizing the United States, the attack served to unite the American nation as no previous disaster ever had. Besides, the raiders left untouched vital oil storage and repair facilities that proved essential in the task of recovery. Unluckily too for the Japanese, three U.S. aircraft carriers were at sea and escaped damage. In a few months their role was vital in carrying the offensive against the Japanese.

In both the U.S. and Canada, however, there was a more immediate
offensive against Japanese living in California and British Columbia,
many of whom were bona fide citizens of their respective countries.
But as events rapidly transpired, citizenship was no guarantee of pro-
tection for any Japanese living in Canada whether Canadian born or
naturalized.

The Pearl Harbor attack (always referred to as a "sneak" attack
rather than a military surprise attack) become the final justification
that set into motion government machinery launching the greatest
forced exodus in the nation's history. Within months of Pearl Harbor,
22,000 Japanese men, women and children along the entire west coast
were uprooted from their homes, jobs and schools and banished to
internment camps of tar-paper shacks in the B.C. interior or to isolated
farming communities elsewhere. There, until the end of the war, they
lived in a limbo of the dispossessed, a frightening suspension of civil
rights worthy of Nazism, ignited by racial hate, and carried out for
political convenience. Any hope on the part of the Japanese Canadians
for fairness or justice was entirely futile. The order-in-council on February 24, 1942, authorizing the mass relocation of the Japanese under
the powers of the War Measures Act, came on the recommendation
of Mackenzie King, whose own record in dealing with Orientals was
a long and questionable one, dating back to 1907.

As the twenty-five-year-old deputy minister of labour, he had been
sent to Vancouver to investigate claims for damages suffered by Japanese Canadians in a race riot. A mob of 5,000 had descended on
Cordova and Powell streets in Vancouver's "Little Tokyo" (or "Jap
Town" as it was also known), breaking windows and smashing the
ghetto's store-fronts. King's solution to ensure future calm was a recommendation to curb emigration from Japan, which the Japanese government agreed to do. In 1923, King accepted a recommendation from
John Oliver, the B.C. premier, to restrict the number of Chinese immigrants applying to enter Canada. In 1928, again on a request from
Oliver, King made another deal with Japan to limit to a mere 150
people the number of Japanese allowed to emigrate to Canada.

In the 1935 federal election, Liberals mounted a blatantly racist
campaign against the C.C.F. Party, suggesting a vote for C.C.F. was

like giving "the Chinamen and the Japanese the same voting right as you have."[1] Two years earlier, the C.C.F. in its Regina manifesto had called for equal treatment before the law for all residents of Canada, regardless of race or creed. As late as January 1941, almost a full year before Pearl Harbor, King banned Canadian citizens of Japanese ancestry from joining the armed forces.

King's dismal record in dealing with aliens was not confined only to Orientals. In response to European immigrants, especially Jews, King, his Cabinet and bureaucrats steadfastly pursued a policy restricting their passage into Canada. Irving Abella and Harold Troper, in their disturbing account of Jewish immigration, *None Is Too Many*, reminded readers "what Canadian history books do not mention and what few Canadians talk about—because they don't know, or worse, don't care—is that, of all the nations of the Western world, of all the states that could have received refugees, theirs was arguably, the worst record for providing sanctuary to European Jewry."[2]

In view of King's attitude toward Chinese and Japanese emigration, Abella's and Troper's indictment, however shocking, was no surprise. King, forever the astute intrepreter of public opinion, certainly followed his instincts in dealing with minority rights. While Canada today generally pursues an enlightened immigration policy, King's Canada of the 1930s was openly intolerant of aliens, especially Orientals in British Columbia, and Jews just about everywhere. "Kikes, Hebs, and Jew boy" were common words in the vernacular of the day. Clubs were exclusive, meaning they excluded Jews and other non-Anglos, including French Canadians. The most exclusive club of all, the Rideau Club of Ottawa, headed the list barring membership to Asians and non-gentiles. It was no different either in most of Canada's golf and country clubs. No single group in Canadian society is more aware of government immigration policy than is the alien resident, as much now as then.

As war clouds gathered in Europe, the Japanese Canadians were certainly aware of newspaper headlines tracking the voyage of the doomed ship, *St. Louis*. In June 1939, the ship found itself limping along the Atlantic seaboard looking for a safe haven to land more than 900 Jewish passengers who were fleeing Nazi Germany. Although they had acquired entrance visas to Cuba, when the ship arrived in Havana authorities changed their mind and refused them permission to disembark. So did four neighbouring Central and Latin American countries. Their only hope was the United States or Canada. A leading group of Canadian gentiles appealed to Ottawa to allow the Jews entry to Canada. King, who was in Washington accompanying the royal family on their visit to the U.S., deflected the plea to Lapointe and Frederick Blair, director of immigration, in Ottawa. Lapointe was hardly an honest broker. As King's Quebec lieutenant it was he who apprised the prime minister on the province's well-known anti-Semitic sentiments and the delicate political manoeuvring required to pacify Quebec's recalcitrant elements of the church, the intelligentsia and the rabble. One may safely assume that recommending a boatload of Jews be allowed to land in Canada was not in the cards. Blair was a worse mediator. A severe, narrow-minded bigot, definitively exposed in *None Is Too Many*, Blair was totally insensitive to the plight of Jewish refugees at any time. He was a man who strictly enforced immigration law, most of which he himself drafted. His position was irrevocable. No country, Blair said, could "open its door wide enough to take in the hundreds of thousands of Jewish people who want to leave Europe: The line must be drawn somewhere."[3] The *St. Louis* steamed back to Europe where many of the passengers were doomed to die in Hitler's death camps.

Was King himself anti-Semitic? Despite his constant and sanctimonious avowals of brotherly love, King repeatedly took no action in the face of frequent and urgent pleas in the late 1930s to allow desperate European Jews entry into Canada, especially so after the infamous *Kristallnacht*. On the evening of November 9, 1938, the Nazis embarked on a campaign of terror against Jews in Germany and Austria. Jewish homes, businesses and synagogues were plundered and put to the torch. Dozens were killed and thousands were hauled off to concentration camps. Yet, despite his decision to do nothing, King's diary contains frequent expressions of sympathy toward Jews and admiration for many Jewish individuals. He did personally intervene on behalf of H. Carl Goldenberg, a young Montreal lawyer, in helping to get Goldenberg's elderly uncle and aunt out of Nazi-occupied

Austria. In this instance, King responded quickly and compassionately. King, however, showed no such token compassion in dealing with Japanese Canadians. King's reputation as a reformer and humanitarian was in direct contrast to his action during the Japanese evacuation, and prompted Thomas R. Berger, the jurist, to write that "whenever he was called upon to support his principles with respect to the Japanese-Canadians, he gave way before the strident calls for measures against them—restriction, evacuation, confiscation and deportation."[4]

Clearly, King's political instincts were sharpened by the mood of the times in the wake of Pearl Harbor and the defeat at Hong Kong. He recognized, too, a smouldering fear by many British Columbians not only of Japanese Canadians but all Asians, and an unhappy history of prejudice stretching back into the nineteenth century. By the turn of the century, Orientals made up ten per cent of British Columbia's population, creating apprehension, resentment and fear among whites that the immigrants were prepared to accept low wages and take away jobs. "The competition for jobs was felt mainly by the working class," said Berger, "but all classes in British Columbia felt that the burgeoning Oriental population represented a long-term threat to the White Character of the province."[5] The bombs and torpedoes dropped from the Mitsubishi and Kawasaki assault planes over Pearl Harbor only confirmed the long, seething suspicion held by many in the white community: The "Jap" was treacherous.

The cry to round up the Japanese Canadians was loud and widespread, from working fishermen to federal members of Parliament, and headed by the most vocal MP Howard Green, the Conservative member for Vancouver South. Green, who later became the minister for external affairs in the government of John Diefenbaker, remained convinced throughout his life that King, the Cabinet and Parliament had acted properly during the hysteria that promoted internment.

> At that time there were about 12 hundred fishing vessels on the coast, and there were nearly 3,000 fishing licences held by Japanese. And they were scattered along the coast. Some of them were powerful enough to cross the Pacific. It was obviously very easy for Japanese naval men to infiltrate through this fleet. I'd

heard many rumours of naval officers being fishermen in the
Japanese vessels. Now, that would not be the majority of them,
but I had no doubt that this was the case, because it happened
everywhere the Japanese troops landed. There was no reason to
think that we would be treated any differently than other countries
which were attacked.

And the Japanese people, most of them no doubt were perfectly
loyal, but they couldn't very well inform on the others. It could
have been a matter of life and death. If the Japanese Army had
invaded Vancouver Island, or had invaded Prince Rupert, there
would have been thousands of Canadians with their throats cut,
just a terrible situation.

I don't think that any Canadian public man would face the
possibility of that without doing something about it.[6]

The bureaucrats moved with uncharacteristic swiftness. Within a
week of Pearl Harbor, all fishing boats were seized. Within a month
all Japanese fishing licences were revoked, whether the fishermen were
citizens or not. Conveniently, the action eliminated the source of a
long-standing complaint of white fishermen that the Japanese were
taking over. "At a stroke," said Berger, "the Japanese Canadians had
finally been removed from the fishing industry."[7] In February 1942,
King expressed impatience, saying, "I feel, too, we have been too
slow in getting the Japanese population moved in B.C."[8]

By the summer of '42, the evacuation was in full swing. Japanese
Canadians, often with only a half-day's notice, were told to pack their
belongings. Each person was allowed one suitcase. At Hastings Park,
site of the Pacific National Exhibition, the evacuees were herded into
the Forum, the overflow steered to the livestock barns. Grace Tucker,
a church worker who visited one Japanese family, remembered, "They
were herded like cattle. When I went to visit this family, it said 'First
Prize Hereford Bull' — that's the stall they were in."[9] While waiting
for trains to take them inland, they were photographed, fingerprinted
and identified by number. In material terms, the Japanese lost everything: land, houses, automobiles, businesses, personal possessions.
They also lost their dignity. At the relocation camps, as the government called them, they lived in shacks covered with tar paper, two
families sharing a space that measured 14' × 24'. At first, there was

no electricity. The huts were not insulated; the only heat was from wood-burning stoves. The Rev. Gordon Nakayama, an Anglican clergyman who was interned, remembered the winter's extreme cold. "A person had put a hot water bottle in their bed and in the morning it was frozen."[10] As the cold penetrated the flimsy huts, exposed nail heads inside frosted over like so many white buttons. Anyone who resisted internment was hauled off to a real concentration camp at Angler, Ontario, where the prisoners wore large red circles painted on their coats.

During these years of shame and frustration, there was not one charge of espionage laid against the Japanese. This is not surprising since the RCMP, the army and the navy all reported that the Japanese community posed no threat whatsoever. In fact the army fears were "concern for the security of the Japanese, not for the security of Canada" and that "the white population might go down en masse to the little town of Steveston and beat up the Japanese," remembered General Maurice Pope.[11] While there was no doubt that the Japanese consulate in Vancouver carried out intelligence-gathering operations, a traditional practice of all foreign missions, and that a handful of Japanese were quickly rounded up and arrested hours after the attack on Pearl Harbor, the irrefutable fact remained that not a single suspect was ever convicted of spying.

In the modern era of heightened concern for civil liberties and for the Charter of Rights and Freedoms, it is of course astonishing that the government acted in such a manner. King solved the problem that the Japanese Canadians posed by their presence with expediency rather than compassion. With the stroke of a pen, he sent them into exile.

The situation wasn't helped, either, by one program in the National Film Board series, *The World in Action*. At the height of the evacuation, the producers released *Mask of Nippon*, an odious piece of documentary cinema with a provocative script. "The soldiers of the Rising Sun are little men, quick and wiry; their uniforms are slovenly, their faces even in the heat of battle are tawny masks, black, expressionless. They believe that they have embarked upon a holy war, a war of liberation."[12] The film showed a sequence of soldiers beating, killing and burying people alive "and the grisly bayoneting of a child to a background chorus of women's shrieks.'' Tom Daly, the doyen of the NFB, years later admitted the footage came from a feature film and that the ''baby'' was probably a doll. Of course, Canadians at the time were unaware of this propaganda.

Perhaps no aspect of the whole affair was as shabby as King's earlier refusal to allow the Japanese Canadians to enlist in the Canadian forces, said Berger. ''The United States had established an all-Japanese unit, the 442 Regimental Combat team, which served with distinction in Europe. King refused to hear of such a thing for Canada until finally, in the spring of 1945, and by special British request, he allowed 150 Nisei to enlist in the Canadian Intelligence Corps to serve as interpreters for Allied units in Southeast Asia.''[13]

The blackest moment came when the government attempted to deport as many Japanese Canadians as it could. While the War Measures Act* had given the government authority to round up the Japanese community, there was no authority to deport its members. Parliament enacted the National Emergency Transitional Powers Act, and the Cabinet passed orders-in-council to deport all Japanese Canadians who asked to be ''repatriated'' to Japan earlier during the war. ''King's policy would make these Japanese Canadians a people without a country,'' said Berger. ''His insensitivity to the enormity of his government's action was complete.''[14] Had the repatriation been carried out, more than 10,000 Japanese Canadians, two-thirds of them Canadian citizens, would have been shipped to Japan. In face of mounting pressure from Canadians outside of British Columbia, King reversed his decision and halted the mass deportations. Still, 4,000 persons had left for Japan.

In 1976, Howard Green was asked if, in hindsight, he would have acted differently. His answer was an emphatic ''no!'' Of the shameful episode, Pickersgill was to say years later, ''It's one of the most horrible facts of war, this business of locking people up, not because they're

---

*The notorious War Measures Act was finally wiped from the books July 21, 1988, when a new Emergencies Act was given royal assent. The government will still have extraordinary powers in times of emergency, except to impose conscription. It is said that the new Emergencies Act ensures civil rights will never again be suspended as they were during World War II when Japanese Canadians were resettled.

guilty of something, but because they might be a danger. But, I suppose as long as we're silly enough to go on having wars, it's a necessary concomitant."[15]

King himself never expressed any doubt about the necessity or the propriety of the mass evacuation and later deportations, confiding to his diary that he had acted justly and with mercy. But the light in which he regarded Asians generally, and Japanese Canadians in particular, was reflected in his remarks following the news of the atomic bombing of Hiroshima. It was fortunate, King wrote in his diary, that the atomic bomb was used on the Japanese rather than on "the white races of Europe."[16]*

All that was in the future. Equally taking King's time and energy in the wake of Pearl Harbor and the demanding logistics involved to carry out the evacuation of the Japanese, was the renewed presence in King's life of his oldest political foe, Arthur Meighen. The austere and ascetic former Conservative prime minister suddenly had returned from the wilderness of the Senate to once more rally his Tory forces. To King it was a direct challenge to his wartime leadership, and it came from a man he detested and feared "to the edge of absurdity."[17]

While the problem of the evacuation of Japanese Canadians was admittedly a large one, King viewed Arthur Meighen as a greater menace, and not one that could be disposed of by orders-in-council. He'd have to be eliminated by other means.

The Japanese Canadians were unfortunate victims of war; Arthur Meighen was a menace.

---

*After the war, the Canadian government offered compensation to Japanese Canadians, but amounts that were considered niggardly even by such public figures as Mr. Green who promoted relocation. At this writing, the National Association of Japanese-Canadians continues to lobby the present government for additional compensation, $25,000 for each survivor of the 22,000. This numbers about 14,000 Japanese Canadians. In addition, the association wants a lump sum of $50 million to put into a community-controlled fund for scholarships and memorials. Also, in May 1987, Canadian veterans imprisoned by the Japanese at Hong Kong filed a $13 million claim for compensation at the United Nations. The claim seeks about $10,000 per person for the 768 Hong Kong veterans still surviving and 200 widows.

CHAPTER SIX

King's Nemesis

MACKENZIE KING'S DARKEST HOUR followed the dawn of the war's second year. In November 1941, the old lion of Quebec politics, Ernest Lapointe, was dying. Cardin was ailing. Ralston, meticulous to the point of fault, showed signs of cracking under pressure. Chubby Power continued hitting the bottle.

The litany of sorrow had begun in June. Like the black violent thunderstorms that lash the Gatineau Hills, a different kind of storm crashed around King on June 15. Little Pat, his cherished terrier and faithful pet of seventeen years, died in his master's arms that June morning up at Kingsmere. King's grief was fevered. One historian described King's reaction as repulsive. But was it? The dog had been his best friend.

As dawn broke, King lay in bed with Pat in his arms, and sang a hymn, "God be with you till we meet again."[1] At five minutes past 5:00, "his little heart seemed to cease." King cuddled the still warm body in his arms for well over an hour. "My little friend, the truest friend I have had — or man ever had," King recorded in his diary,

74

adding he "felt a great peace when all was ended," and thanked God for answering his prayers to let Pat die in his arms. Outside, a chorus of birds sang, a squirrel clamoured in a tree, and a crow flew low past the house, cawing three times to announce the proclamation of death, as King interpreted this flight. King was also filled with guilt, blaming himself for lingering over a second Scotch a few days earlier, rather than rushing home to be with the ailing dog. He vowed then to renounce forever the use of alcohol. "I prayed God to accept my vow," and that he "might give my best wholly to His service — to keep this as a memorial to Pat — that I may do my great work for mankind." While affinity with the Deity motivated him in most things in his life, King did not forsake demon rum.

The month of August was little better. King flew to England late in the month, aboard a liberator bomber whose interior had been turned into a tiny apartment with a divan. At Aldershot, southwest of London, where King had gone to review Canadian troops, some of the soldiers booed their wartime prime minister. It was an incident that got wide press coverage at home, a protest the Tories interpreted as being one against King's stand not to enforce overseas conscription. A more likely explanation was the fact the troops had stood for more than an hour in a cold rain waiting for King who was late.

By September 10, King was back in Canada reporting to the War Cabinet, which was itself wrestling with the growing conscription issue. At this time, King admitted he began to wilt under the pressure. He said November 8 was one of his most trying days, adding that he was "sick at heart [and] wanted to give up public life and avoid the break in my health which I feared might come. The strain is terrible —mental fatigue and physical combined, but depression as well, and feeling of being left alone, old colleagues gone or going, no one to help, and alone at Laurier House . . . no one to talk with."[2]

King's disconsolate mood was due in great part to the presence on the horizon of his oldest and most hated political enemy, the severe and righteous Arthur Meighen. All that autumn, Tories had been pressuring Meighen to leave his safe Senate seat, take over the reins of a shattered Conservative Party, present himself as a candidate for the House of Commons, and challenge King over his refusal to bring in

overseas conscription. As everyone remembered, the former prime
minister was the only politician who ever penetrated King's defences.
The mere thought of having to face this formidable opponent again
left King shaking with fear and rage, a condition that Hutchison found
the prime minister in one day at Laurier House. Pacing his office as
if in a cage, King charged Meighen with being "the most reactionary
and disruptive element(s) in Canadian life."[3] He pounded his desk,
clenched his fist, yelling that Meighen's return to daily politics was
"nothing less than the beginning of Fascism in Canada." Hutchison
was taken aback by this performance from someone who never visibly
lost control of his emotions. "This childish outburst, so unlike King,
seemed meaningless and inane," said Hutchison, "but its meaning
was very simple. King could not tolerate Meighen's presence as a man
near him in Parliament. He could not manage the war with Meighen's
presence as a statesman and as a conscriptionist."

The King-Meighen feud was a long one, worth examining. Arthur
Meighen was born in 1874 (the same year as King) in St. Mary's, a
drowsy town in southwestern Ontario. His parents, thrifty Presby-
terians, shared the "Victorian belief in progress, a belief that man
was capable of and was undergoing both material and moral improve-
ment,"[4] a belief that established institutions of church, family and
school "would provide the foundation for change and would be
strengthened by it." Meighen and King first met as fellow students
at the University of Toronto, but there is no evidence either one
regarded the other with animosity. That came later. After university,
Meighen moved to Portage La Prairie where he decided on a career
in law, serving a successful apprenticeship at several firms before being
called to the Manitoba bar. He married a school teacher in 1904 and
decided three years later to run as a Conservative candidate in the
1908 general election. He won. By 1913, Meighen was appointed
solicitor general in the Borden government. By 1920, Meighen had
succeeded Sir Robert as prime minister. At age forty-five, Meighen
had become the youngest prime minister in the country's history. But
in December 1921, he fell from power, losing to Mackenzie King,
who was Laurier's heir as leader of the Liberal party. Although
Meighen also lost his own seat in that election, another was found for

him and for the next four years in Opposition he became a torment to King in Parliament. He had also gained the reputation of a patriot and a hard-liner. During World War I, it was Meighen who introduced legislation banning aliens from voting, and during the Winnipeg strike in 1919 he drafted amendments to the Criminal Code that were seen as regressive. In Opposition, Meighen was merciless in his attacks on King who "was pestered, ridiculed and frustrated."[5] Once he taunted the Government benches: "Speak up. Don't behave as your ancestors did ten thousand years ago." The seeds of hate were being sown.

The fierce hate between King and Meighen has been told many times around the campfires of the Liberal tribe.

King, frustrated by four years of minority government, called a general election in 1925, issuing as the battle cry the need for a majority government. He didn't get it. The Liberals ended up with 101 seats, the Tories 116, the Progressives 24. Everyone thought King would hand the government over to Meighen, since he had the most seats. That would have been the conduct becoming an honourable politician. Instead, King convinced Governor-General Viscount Byng that he could carry on with the support of the Progressives. The next six months were chaotic ones with plots and sub-plots that not even a movie script-writer could invent. Soon, the Conservatives exposed corruption in the customs department. King, seeking to avoid a censure vote that was inevitable, approached Byng again and admitted he couldn't govern after all, asking the governor-general for a dissolution and a new election. When Byng refused, King resigned. Meighen was asked to form a makeshift government, which he did. However, under the law existing at the time, Meighen could not sit in Parliament without being re-elected in his own constituency. It was a ludicrous situation. The prime minister was reduced to watching the melodrama from the public galleries while a cabinet of so-called ministers on the floor below tried to keep his Conservative government on the rails. Then, without warning, King accused Byng of defying parliament when he had refused King's earlier request for dissolution. Further, King said, Meighen was governing illegally. When Parliament came to decide the issue, King's Opposition squeaked by with a single vote. On September 14, 1926, Canadians went to the polls, and the Liberals won just enough seats to form a government. Meighen vanished into Bay Street, emerging in 1932 to accept a Senate appointment offered by R.B. Bennett, then in power. As far as King was concerned, the Senate was a good place for Meighen. He was out of sight.

So ended the race between the hare and the tortoise. Meighen, who moved rapidly, dramatically and categorically, in the end lost to the man who operated slowly, moderately and ambiguously. They were both arrogant men, but King hid his arrogance much better than Meighen. While the public admired his parliamentary brilliance, it didn't like his rapier tongue. "Meighen had command of the King's English," said Alex Hume, "and he laced it to King no end. King was palsied with fear in the face of Meighen's withering attacks."[6] Someone else said Meighen operated like a surgeon, but in his frenzy he could never bring himself short of anything but complete disembowelment of his victims. Of all the manifold accusations that King might hang around Meighen's neck, there was one thing Meighen never abandoned—candour. Meighen said what he believed. Now in the fall of 1941, Meighen, emerging from his lair in the Senate, was back on the war-path, once more saying what he believed. What he believed was enough to paralyze King with fear.

"I am getting past the time when I can fight in public with a man of Meighen's type who is sarcastic, vitriolic and the meanest type of politician," King grumbled. "Even Bennett was better than Meighen as an opponent."[7] Meighen's fires were certainly spectacular ones, but King's thoroughness in campaign strategy was Teutonic. Besides, King worked longer and harder than ordinary men. As Meighen plotted his campaign, King was deluged with more grief. Ernest Lapointe, the old warrior, died November 26. King was devastated. He and Lapointe had survived shot and shell together for nearly forty years. King visited Lapointe on his deathbed for a tearful farewell. They kissed and clasped hands, and the old fighter slipped away. Almost before the corpse was cold, King was frantic to find a new commander for his Quebec guard. Cardin, who was the natural heir, was ill, too, and suggested Louis St. Laurent, a corporation lawyer who spoke eloquent English and, best of all, did not oppose conscription. Later, the press would dub St. Laurent "Uncle Louie," suggesting a homey

Québécois who sat around a habitant kitchen playing the spoons. In truth he possessed a cold, steely intellect, not unlike one of his eventual successors, Pierre Trudeau. St. Laurent was King's man.

During the closing days of 1941, King's energy level was nothing short of astonishing. Every day he fumed and plotted how to deal with Meighen. Then came Pearl Harbor and the declaration of war against Japan, followed by growing and depressing news about the fate of Canadians in Hong Kong. On Christmas Day he travelled to Washington to meet with Roosevelt and Winston Churchill. Churchill returned to Ottawa with King at the end of the month where he uttered his famous "some chicken, some neck" line in the House of Commons.

Churchill departed and King hunkered down in Ottawa facing 1942 with some apprehension. Ahead lay the new session of Parliament and Meighen's presence on the hustings in Toronto's South York, one of four ridings being contested in by-elections. All this was juxtaposed with the aftermath of events in the Far East, not to mention increased public debate over conscription. But, it was South York that was the time bomb. "He was horrified," said Hutchison. "King worried more about the South York by-election and the possible reappearance of Meighen in the House of Commons, than he ever worried about anything in his life. . . . He was really almost hysterical."[8] And for good reason. Another one of King's detested enemies had now joined Meighen in his campaign to take South York in the February 9 by-election. George Drew, the Ontario Tory party leader, in the first days of 1942 began making waves on Meighen's behalf. No politician ever had so many concrete issues to debate in the campaign battle as did Meighen and his Ontario sidekick, Drew, a man not to be trifled with.

Drew was movie-star handsome, a Hollywood stereotype of a university president with his silver hair, articulate tongue and beautifully tailored suits. In private "he was a warm and friendly human being who loved a party and loved laughter and gaiety."[9] But Drew was slightly handicapped on the public platform where he appeared rather stiff and who, like Brian Mulroney, never knew what to do with his arms. There wasn't much he could do about that. Badly wounded in World War I, Drew's arms hung like two broken sticks, projecting awkwardness. Yet, as a war veteran his credibility was above suspicion in questioning King's performance as the man leading the nation in war. Early in January, Drew began demanding a government accounting of the disaster at Hong Kong, charging it was a powerful argument for conscription. "Let us consider the most terrible example of this shortage of trained men," Drew said. "At the last moment a large number of untrained men were attached to the forces leaving for Hong Kong," many of whom had no weapons training. "What a cruel betrayal of public duty it is for anyone who knows the truth to try to convince the Canadian people that the present system of raising men has not failed, and failed miserably," Drew told his listeners.[10]

To stem the criticism, King quickly moved to defuse Hong Kong and conscription as campaign issues. At the opening of the Parliamentary session on January 22, he cleverly deflected this potential fire by announcing that an inquiry would be held into the facts about the fateful Hong Kong expedition. He also announced that any question of conscription for overseas service should be one that was answered by all Canadians, perhaps in the form of a plebiscite or referendum. With two swift strokes, King cut the heart out of Drew's and Meighen's campaign strategy. The announcement of the plebiscite sent another of King's old foes into the South York fray. Mitch Hepburn suddenly re-emerged. He called the plebiscite "the most dastardly, contemptible, and cowardly thing ever perpetrated on a respected and dignified country by any government."[11] Hepburn, still technically a Liberal, then cast his support behind Meighen and Drew, by whom all help was gratefully accepted.

While the federal Liberals, with gentlemanly grace, did not put up a candidate in South York—a gesture that would put fewer barriers in Meighen's path to re-enter Parliament—they surreptitiously backed Meighen's C.C.F. opponent. Joseph W. Noseworthy was going to need all the help he could get. The Toronto high-school teacher had run in the 1940 general election but was soundly beaten by his Conservative opponent, Alan Cockeram, the member who resigned so Meighen could contest the seat. Besides, no one but a Conservative had ever won Toronto's South York. It was time money changed hands. Two weeks before election day, Senator Norman Lambert, the Liberal party's crafty bagman, received the strangest of requests. The federal Liberal member, Brooke Claxton, of Montreal's St. Lawrence-St. George riding, asked Lambert if he could immediately come up with $1,000 for Noseworthy. The money was passed to Andrew Brewin, one of Noseworthy's aides. Whether this was all the money the Liberals contributed to the C.C.F. to ensure Meighen's defeat is not known but, given the Liberal's history in funding election campaigns, it is unlikely. What is known is that the Liberal riding machine worked actively on Noseworthy's behalf. Besides, the Liberals started a whispering campaign to discredit Meighen. King's nemesis was touted as having been undemocratically selected as the new Tory leader. There had never been a Conservative party convention to pick Meighen as Tory chief; he had been ramrodded into leadership.

Instead of an election campaign centring on issues, the affair turned into comic opera when Hepburn entered the stage. At one point Hepburn's minister of mines, Robert Laurier, Sir Wilfrid's nephew, told King privately he was going to resign as a protest against Hepburn's support for Meighen. King was delighted but when the election was over Laurier informed King that Hepburn never accepted his resignation. This prompted King, the deadliest of political head-hunters, to condemn Ontario politics as "so amateurish and school-boyish that it makes me rather nauseated."[12]

Meighen himself did not deliver his usual bravura performance. Was he getting too old? Perhaps. The C.C.F. itself was not above delivering low blows either. M.J. Coldwell, the C.C.F. House leader, equated Meighen to Hitler. "I would just as soon live under Hitler as under that man," Coldwell said.[13] The C.C.F. dredged up Meighen's past too, not as a personal vendetta, they said, but only as a review of his record. It turned out that he had sent soldiers overseas in World War I with defective rifles; that he opposed old age pensions; that he suppressed labour organizations. The tactics prompted Roger Graham, Meighen's biographer, to say, "One shudders to think what might have come forth had the C.C.F. decided to attack him personally!"[14] Halfway through the campaign, Meighen confided to his son Ted that "this has been my worst week in years" and that he was "driven like a galley slave, vilified like a low criminal and all for a seat in the House of Commons that I do not want." Still, Meighen drove himself on to the point of exhaustion in a door-to-door campaign until "his voice grew hoarse, his nerves grew taut in this endless, enervating progress from one crowd of people to another." As the campaign neared its end, Meighen himself felt the constituents of South York "would rather welcome Satan than me." Hepburn's support was surely a kiss of death, and the combined campaign might of the Liberals and C.C.F. was too much of a barricade to break through.

Until election day, King himself was uncertain of victory in South York, doubting that the C.C.F. could defeat Meighen. For once his instincts were wrong. Noseworthy crushed Meighen. King was jubilant. Not only had Meighen been defeated, but three Liberals, including St. Laurent, running in other by-elections, were victorious. On February 9, 1942, Mackenzie King added two more scalps to his growing collection; Meighen's and Drew's would hang beside those of Hepburn, Duplessis and Manion.

King, who was never magnanimous in victory, was no different that evening as he sat in Laurier House putting his emotions on paper. "I felt tonight that public life in Canada had been cleansed, as though we have gone through a storm and got rid of something that was truly vile and bad, and which, had it been successful at this time, might have helped to destroy the effectiveness of our war effort."[15] And, as Roger Graham reminded his readers in Meighen's biography, King credited his triumph over the forces of evil to that divine power with which he was ever in holy alliance. "I felt most grateful to Providence for what Canada has been spared of division and strife," wrote King, before turning off the lights and retiring to bed.

So ended the hate-filled saga of Mackenzie King and Arthur Meighen, a feud so bitter that the Meighen family remembered it for years after with something less than charity. Meighen's widow recalled running into King at a country club at a society function. As the party broke up, King put his arm around Mrs. Meighen saying, "I'll be taking this dear girl home."[16] "Thanks," she said. "I have the car." When asked if that was as close as she ever got to the prime minister, she replied, "It was as close as I ever wanted to get."

Mackenzie King's sense of a divine mission took him to Nazi Germany in 1937 to meet Hitler. King was the only leader of the allied cause to do so.
PA-119013

Ernest Lapointe, Minister of Justice and King's Quebec lieutenant. A powerful influence on King, Lapoint dies in 1941.
National Archives of Canada C-26553

King and his beloved Irish terrier, Pat. King had three terriers in his lifetime, all named Pat. It was Pat no. 1 he most revered. King was devastated when the pet died.

King signs the Order-in-council that sends 22,000 Japanese-Canadians, many of them
citizens, to camps in the interior of British Columbia in the summer of 1942.
King offers no regrets over the decision.

Public Archives of Canada C-46356

*Charles Gavan 'Chubby' Power,
King's Minister for Air, resigns
from Cabinet after King reverses
himself and imposes overseas
conscription. He is seen here with
Louis St. Laurent, left, who
supported conscription and
succeeded King as prime minister.*

Public Archives of Canada C-23549

Gen. A.G.L. 'Andy' McNaughton, sometimes called the father of the Canadian Army, replaces J.L. Ralston as Minister of Defence. He shocks the fighting men when he supports King on the conscription issue. Shortly, he changes his mind and recommends sending 'Zombies' into battle.

Public Archives of Canada C-54548

C.D. Howe, Minister of Munitions and Supply, is blunt and tough in his efforts to get Canadian war industry into high gear. Here Edna Poirier presents Howe with the 100,000,000th, 25-pounder shell produced in a plant in Cherrier, Quebec.

Public Archives of Canada C-7487

Mitch Hepburn, left, Ontario's playboy premier, challenges Mackenzie King's wartime leadership and loses the fight.

Ontario Archives S-304

King takes time out to escort movie star Shirley Temple at a Victory Bond Rally on Parliament Hill. Her visit comes at the height of the bitter debate within Cabinet on whether Canada should impose conscription for overseas service.

National Archives of Canada C-29451

Gen. H.D.G. 'Harry' Crerar is involved in decisions that send Canadians into battle in Hong Kong and Dieppe, both of which are military disasters.

National Archives of Canada PA-140409

Mackenzie King, Franklin Delano Roosevelt and Winston Churchill at the Quebec Conference, August 1943. King plays the role of mediator between the American president and the British prime minister.

Public Archives of Canada C-14168

James Layton Ralston, Minister of National Defence, investigates reports firsthand that untrained troops and wounded men are being sent into battle because of manpower shortages. Ralston, in trenchcoat, returns from the front in late 1944, igniting the conscription crisis.

National Archives of Canada PA-136824

Mackenzie King visits Canadian battlefields in France, August 1946.
Public Archives of Canada C-4973

Arthur Meighen, former Conservative prime minister, is a life-long and bitter opponent of King's.
Public Archives of Canada C-21438

Meighen's son Max was more frank. In a film interview he was asked about his father's feelings toward King. He hissed one short sentence: "He despised him."[17] Despite Meighen's bone-crushing defeat, one of the issues he had hammered home during the dirty by-election campaign simply would not go away. Conscription.

CHAPTER SEVEN

First Crisis Averted

MACKENZIE KING UTTERED TWO memorable phrases in his lifetime. In 1929, under the gun in the House of Commons for paltry relief payments to the Depression-gripped provinces — some with Tory administrations — King promised he "would not give a single cent to any Tory government."[1] Amidst R.B. Bennett's howl of "Shame!" King put his foot further in his mouth. "May I repeat what I have said? . . . I would not give them a five-cent piece!" This was King's famous "five-cent speech" remark that helped him lose the 1930 election. Forevermore, King speeches were cautious ones, avoiding all occasions requiring improvisation.

Such was the case in the winter and spring of 1942 when any declaration regarding conscription demanded ambiguity. Although King had masterfully side-stepped answering English Canada's growing cry for overseas conscription during the South York by-election, the situation following the April 27 plebiscite reached a climax. That night Canada, although not Quebec, had voted overwhelmingly to give King and Parliament the authority to impose conscription if need be. The vote surprised no one, but the electors must have stared with some confusion when first faced with the question of the plebiscite. The simple question, "written in King's worst style of sprawling participles," said Hutchison, "but as sound in politics as it was weak in construction,"[2] asked the voters the following: "Are you in favour of releasing the Government from any obligation arising out of any past commitments restricting the methods of raising men for military service?" Sixty-four per cent of Canadians answered yes, but the figure was anything but evenly spread across the country. In Quebec, seventy-six per cent returned a resounding no!

King, ensconced in his library at Laurier House, listened to the early returns on radio. By midnight it was clear that the plebiscite had given the Government and Parliament a free hand. King was also aware of the disparity between the English and French vote, that the governing "factor was racial, and possibly race and religion combined."[3] While he sifted through the information in his mind, King concluded, "I felt very strongly that to keep Canada united we would have to do all in our power from reaching the point where necessity for conscription for overseas would arise."

The decision, made on a rainy April night, would have fateful results in two years' time. For the moment, however, King faced an enormous and more immediate challenge on his own doorstep: the Cabinet itself was split on the issue. Tension, stress and extreme fatigue created the worst kind of atmosphere. Layton Ralston, as defence minister, was a super-conscriptionist. In fact, Ralston's immediate reaction to the plebiscite results was his belief that he could start calling up every able-bodied Canadian in the country. Cardin was adamantly opposed. Power, now minister for air, was equally bewildered. Hadn't they all proclaimed in public to Quebecers there'd be no conscription! And if it ever happened, they'd all quit.

During May and early June, Mackenzie King was never better as the mediator, manipulator and soother of emotions. He was at his persuasive best, motivated perhaps by a vision he had experienced the night of the plebiscite. He dreamed he was holding two curved stone pillars and "was seeking to weld them together."[4] He awoke before succeeding but was convinced the two pillars represented English and

French Canada, the ''two elements of the population.'' He'd need all the glue there was just to keep his Cabinet from coming apart. The worst case was Ralston. Over a period of weeks, Ralston threatened to think of resigning; then threatened to resign; and finally resigned. The resignation, however, was never accepted by King. Instead, he pocketed it, making sure all bases were covered in an eventual showdown in the future. More pressing, however, was that some kind of statement was needed to both pacify English Canada who thought a yes vote meant conscription, and be equally reassuring to French Canadians that their no vote was being given rightful consideration in the halls of power in Ottawa.

The time had come for inspired words. The opportunity presented itself June 10, 1942, the day Parliament was to debate Bill 80. As a result of the plebiscite, King wanted to remove a clause in the National Resources Mobilization Act, giving the government authority to impose unlimited conscription if the war situation became serious enough to warrant such drastic measures. Adding to the taut atmosphere was Cardin's sudden resignation. The palpable tension had to be, at the least, diffused or neutralized.

On June 9, King laboured over the speech he would deliver the next day in the Commons. With him was Jack Pickersgill, at this stage the number-two man in King's prime ministerial sanctum. Pickersgill was a young former university professor whose acerbic tongue and incisive mind combined to make him a lethal weapon in political battle. That night, after Pickersgill departed, King scribbled in his diary his most famous words, his most celebrated phrase — ''not necessarily conscription but conscription if necessary.''[5] King was not the author; neither was Pickersgill. He too had plagiarized them, passing the phrase on to a desperate prime minister. Had he not, the most memorable words in Canadian political history would never have been uttered. How Pickersgill happened to be with King that evening is a story in itself.

John Whitney Pickersgill had arrived in Ottawa at age thirty-two, joining an élite group of eighteen other youthful public servants who had been hand-picked and recruited by the resident guru in the department of external affairs, Oscar Douglas Skelton. Pickersgill and his companions were to become Ottawa's first mandarins, the vanguard of the capital's powerful, privileged and influential bureaucrats who made pushing paper an art.

Pickersgill had arrived in Ottawa from Winnipeg in late 1937. At first his duties were not demanding ones, and he idled away his time in an attic office in the East Block reading *The New York Times*. Within two months, Pickersgill was assigned to the PMO where he was told by a colleague, "You don't need to worry . . . you'll only last six weeks. Nobody lasts longer than that."[6] From 1938 on, Pickersgill became King's right hand, composing speeches and public statements, and preparing official correspondence. By war's end the young Manitoban with the goofy grin was running the prime minister's office.

As King's chief speech-writer, Pickersgill discovered King was a perfectionist when it came to putting words on paper and "that nothing was routine to which he signed his name, and the simplest letter of congratulation or message of sympathy was revised with the same painstaking care as the most important speech or state paper."[7] It was not easy being King's ghost writer, in part because King's quasi-Victorian attitudes were often inhibiting. Pickersgill was never allowed to use the word "challenge" because King said it was a word that might be found on a YMCA brochure. "Decent" was another word that was banned because it suggested indecent. Pickersgill obtained a BBC style book on how to write speeches for radio; never use a subordinate clause, the book said. Never use pronouns. Don't repeat a phrase; each sentence should stand on its own.

On the night of June 9, 1942, Pickersgill was going to need all his creative talents in preparing King's address that was to be given to the House the following day, perhaps the most important since the war began. The speech was to be a concrete statement regarding government policy on conscription in the wake of the plebiscite results. No extreme view would be permitted. As Pickersgill told Sigmund Brouwer, a graduate student, the memorable line that was written into the final draft wasn't his at all. Pickersgill had brought to Laurier House with him that night a file of notes and clippings, including one from the Toronto *Star*, an editorial that had appeared on April 28, 1942, the day after the plebiscite. Someone had clipped it for

Pickersgill. "I gave Mr. King the clipping," he told Brouwer.[8] "When he read this thing, he read it twice and then he looked up at me and said, 'I'm going to put this in my speech!' That's how that celebrated phrase started. It became part of the folklore of Canada."

The editorial began: "Not necessarily conscription, but conscription if necessary—that is the significance of Canada's overwhelming 'Yes' vote on the plebiscite."[9]

The new promise satisfied all factions, conscriptionists, Quebec, and both Ralston and Power. In silencing Ralston, King complained of the man's obstinacy that caused him more headaches "than all the problems put together."[10] One problem was solved. Ralston decided to stay on as defence minister. Power, too, convinced himself that the phrase did not compromise his vow to French Canada.

On May 7, ten days after the plebiscite, King told the Cabinet the time had come to amend the National Resources Mobilization Act. Specifically he recommended repealing Section 3 of the Act to remove the prohibition against overseas conscription. He reminded Cabinet that this did not mean automatic conscription for overseas. If the war situation suddenly demanded that possibility, then the government could make the decision and Parliament could judge the decision by a vote of confidence. Only Cardin left the Cabinet and kept his word to Quebecers. Ill with cancer, no one expected him to survive the war. However, Cardin undertook a vigorous campaign to undermine King's leadership until the very end, as the leader of a small coterie of breakaway Quebec Liberal *separatistes*. As far as King was concerned, despite the man's silken voice and splendid suits, Cardin suffered delusions created by an inferiority complex. His departure, as King rightly concluded, was not that damaging after all.

Bill 80 (which took its name from its number on the order paper) passed second reading in Parliament on July 7, 158 to 54. It was not surprising that the dissenters included forty-five Quebec Liberals. King was heartened but his mood, and that of all Canadians that summer, was grim.

Famous words and memorable slogans were not going to be enough to save the world. The summer of 1942 was heavy with the air of defeat. Hitler's legions held all of Europe and were poised at the

outskirts of Leningrad and Moscow. Rommel's Afrika Korps had captured Tobruk. German U-boats roamed the oceans from Norway to
Brazil. In the Mediterranean, tiny Malta, starving and bleeding, was
under an aerial seige by the Luftwaffe. In the Pacific, the news was
worse. Bataan and Corregidor had fallen. In Burma, the British army
beat a hasty retreat from Rangoon in the face of the advancing Japanese,
who also invaded New Guinea, a country ominously close to Australia.
The day Parliament passed Bill 80, the Japanese invaded the Western
Aleutian Islands. It was convincing proof to Mackenzie King that more
Canadian soldiers shouldn't be sent to Europe; they'd need to be kept
at home to defend Canada. The only respite was news of the Battle
of Midway where a rejuvenated U.S. navy mauled the Japanese fleet,
although at the time it wasn't clear to the public how great a victory
had been won. Besides, the situation was so oppressive everywhere
else in the world, Midway couldn't overshadow the Nazis' spectacular
advances from the Steppes of Russia to the sands of North Africa.

Just as important, profound changes were reshaping the face of
Canada. On the battlefront, the country's innocence of youth was being
put to the test for the second time since the beginning of the century.
On the home front, the nation that had gone to war as a rural society
had now become in a few short years an industrial power of immense
complexity.

King and Canada's war had become two struggles, one to adapt,
the other to survive.

PART III

THE DARKEST NIGHT, THE BRIGHTEST DAWN
August 1942– August 1944

CHAPTER EIGHT

The Sailor's War

T

HE SEA HAS MANY moods and Canadian sailors came to know them all: benign, petulant, angry and destructively violent. While there were times when the penetrating beauty of the sea might have left indelible impressions, it was mostly a grim, hostile environment in which thousands of young Canadians suddenly found themselves—right from the beginning of the war. They discovered soon enough, too, that the sea demanded constant and continuing respect, and that the slightest lapse meant terrible retribution. Added to the fearful conditions was the ever present enemy who, contrary to poster propaganda, was not a blockhead stuffed with wurst and beer. He was aggressive, dedicated and thoroughly trained. Of all the Canadian fighting services in World War II, the Royal Canadian Navy was in over its head from the first shot and, not surprisingly, experienced many failures. No service suffered as much anguish in birth or such sustained discomfort in adolescence.

When war broke out, the RCN fleet consisted of seven smoke-belching destroyers, a handful of patrol vessels and a few harbour boats. These were manned by fewer than 2,000 officers and men. On

September 19, 1939, King's cabinet approved an ambitious program to construct 110 ships. Incredibly, by the end of the war Canada had built nearly ten times that number of merchant ships and naval vessels, a shipbuilding feat that was "probably the most remarkable even of the three great naval powers."[1]

In achieving this production miracle there were enormous risks involved, the greatest perhaps being the shipbuilders themselves. Very few yards had ever built anything larger than 100'. An even bigger risk was the decision to concentrate on building an untried design for escort vessels. At the beginning, the British Admiralty simply called it a patrol vessel, whaler type. Later the design was given a more pugnacious name. The world and the enemy came to know the ship as a corvette, a jaunty and nimble fighting ship whose crews came to both curse and love it. Hollywood even made a movie about the corvettes and the Canadians who took them into action. The movie script avoided any mention of the countless problems the builders faced. To begin with, shipyards were forced to expand and as production quotas multiplied, new yards had to be built from scratch. Because of the urgent timetable, short cuts were common. Instead of building conventional and expensive slipways, where the boat was launched stern first, the corvettes were launched sideways. If a child with a toy boat could do this in the bathtub, why not a real ship?

Hiring enough skilled shipworkers was another problem. Some hiring practices became innovative if not devious. One shipyard superintendent always asked prospective riveters if they had ever played softball. If the answer was yes, their employment was assured. He saw a parallel in the rhythm shown by a riveting team. The movement of the arm of the man who pitched the hot rivets to the riveter with a pair of tongs was not unlike the motion used by a softball pitcher delivering the ball to the plate. The riveter who caught the pitch (using what looked like a flour scoop) often stretched like a first baseman handling a short throw.

The weather was a liability, too. Both the workers and the ship were exposed to the elements year round. Work went on every day of the week including Sunday, revolving around three shifts.

Space, too, was precious. Instead of using the larger yards in the

Maritimes or Quebec to construct smaller motor patrol boats, family boat-building operators, most of whom were located on the Great Lakes, were contracted by the government to produce fleets of tiny boats. In fact, this may have been the greatest construction miracle of all. Small boat artisans, a characteristically dreamy lot at any time, were traditionally indifferent to production schedules.

But it was the corvette that was the backbone of the RCN. They began rolling off the production line like so many squat little sausages. One hundred and twenty-three corvettes were built in Canada out of a total of 953 ships launched between 1939 and 1945. At the peak of construction, the Canadian shipbuilding industry employed 73,000 workers.

By the end of 1940, the first fourteen corvettes built in Canada were steaming down the St. Lawrence, bound for Britain. Because of a lack of four-inch guns, the ships were rigged with wooden "dummies," to deceive the Germans during the Atlantic crossing. Green lumber and wet sea conditions left the guns drooping in their mounts. A British admiral who watched the ships approach dryly asked his staff if the Canadians were intending to club the enemy to death.

Manning the ships became a training and logistical nightmare because of the dramatic expansion the RCN experienced. In five years, the navy grew fifty times its original size.

In every way, the RCN was a pick-up navy, not unlike some scrub team playing softball on a weedy baseball diamond in any small town in Canada. The analogy is appropriate because that's who the officers and ratings were: bank tellers, hardware store clerks, farmers, office desk jockeys, electricians, plumbers and greasy-spoon short-order cooks. Together, they made up the RCN's second navy, reservists and volunteer reservists who did not have to be legislated or dragooned into battle. They were all volunteers. Therein lay the seeds of conflict between the very few professional officers and ratings, and this rapidly emerging and scruffy lot of amateurs, who almost never looked like the professional's idea of a sailor in their grab-bag mix of sea-going rig that just might include a Toronto Maple Leaf hockey sweater, Grand Banks hip waders and Tip Top Tailor baseball caps.

To the regular RCN officer, who had spent the first five years of his naval career aboard Royal Navy ships of the line in his tailored uniforms from London's Gieves and Hawkes, the creative displays of dress of this ragamuffin navy merely confirmed his worst suspicion of amateurism. More galling, perhaps for the professionals who knew how to make the system operate, they often found themselves desk-bound ashore while the mongrel breed of sailor manned the ships. In their eyes, it was the worst possible situation. The inmates were running the asylum. Worse, because the Canadian regulars had served with the Royal Navy, with its history of severe discipline, when they tried imposing the same kind of rules on these civilians turned sailors, there were immediate problems. The consequence, said James A. Boutilier, was that "young RCN officers absorbed the ethos of a foreign naval service, a world where officers were born to lead and men were born to be led."[2] The book said so. It was a situation that dogged the wartime RCN from the beginning. "Unused to the restrictions and restraints of life in the highly organized societies and huge cities of older cultures," said James B. Lamb, "Canadian youths brought up in the free-and-easy atmosphere of the wide-open spaces and small Canadian towns did not take easily to the confining nature of service life, with its inflexible routine; its insistence on detail; its subservience to author-ity."[3] The situation manifested itself in any number of ways. There was a carefree attitude — old salts would have called it cheekiness — that permeated daily routine, none better illustrated than one incident involving signals at sea. A Canadian warship was steaming into Gibral-tar, that bastion outpost of the British Empire, when it was challenged by a crisp signal from shore.

"What ship?" the Royal Navy flashed toward the incoming Canadians.

"What rock?" came back the reply.[4]

Also, Canadians were not altogether reverent when referring to their ships. Sailors aboard HMCS *Restigouche* called her "Rusty Guts" and the crew of HMCS *Rimouski* always called the ship the "Polish" corvette.

This insouciance occasionally caused greater anguish. In 1943, some disgruntled sailors aboard HMCS *Iroquois* locked themselves in their mess deck, refusing to take watches. The "incident," as the navy decided to call it, was nothing short of mutiny, although at the time, the RCN played down events, fearful of the reaction of the folks back home.

Much of the sailors' unrest was the direct result of intolerable living conditions at sea, especially at the beginning of the war aboard the first newly constructed corvettes, ships that were in the first place never built for long sea voyages anyway. While two families of interned Japanese Canadians found themselves sharing a living space of 24' × 14', as many as thirty Canadian sailors lived, slept, and ate for weeks, months and even years in a space barely larger. To say they slept was an exaggeration. Wrapped like caterpillars in a cocoon, the seamen fell into hammocks slung wherever there was space, almost always fully dressed, hugging a tin hat or life-jacket. Because sea watches were constant, four hours on, four hours off, the rhythm of activity was ceaseless. Noisy, ill-ventilated and forever damp and dripping, shipboard life, particularly in corvettes, was altogether intolerable, just like the monotonous food of corned beef hash and rubbery shepherd's pie. There was never a moment's privacy, and rarely seas calm enough to pacify the squat steel hull. At times, storms were truly fearful and the seas so massive they defied description. In the mid-Atlantic during winter, huge mile-long walls of waves, as high as a five-storey apartment building, snatched a ship like a veritable cork, sucking it skyward in a thunderous rush to such a height that Hugh Garner remembered his fear of the ship foundering was replaced by a "fear of heights."[5] Their constant battle was directed as much against the sea as the enemy. The sea was where fearsome storms caused almost as much damage as German torpedoes, with thousands of tons of water, a force so powerful no technology could ever tame it. The sea was a seething, green mass that often snapped steel stanchions, bent bow plates, or swept away in a micro-second deck gear and rafts bolted to the ship. When the sea and the wind combined to protest, and it didn't matter what ocean or what season, there was nothing to do but ride it out, trying to head into the mountainous swell. A following sea was worse. A ship was propelled forward, as if being lifted on a roller-coaster, exposing the screaming propeller before being flung forward and down another mountainside of water, a manoeuvre that threatened with each plunge to toss the ship end-over-end. Steaming abeam, the monster courted disaster where the avalanche of water tipped the ship to a perilous fifty degrees, virtually lying her on her side.

By all accounts, the run to Murmansk was absolutely the worst of all convoy duty, particularly in December when it was impossible to distinguish night from day even at noon.

A few Canadian warships made three or four convoy runs north of the Arctic Circle to Murmansk, but Charles McLennan, who got there and back aboard HMCS *Stormont*, admitted, "That was quite enough."[6] Of course, there were smoother times and sunny skies, as in the Mediterranean, but the spectre of storms past, while out of sight, were seldom out of mind. Besides, sailors could never agree which was worse, the terrifying sea that reduced enemy submarine attacks, or milk-pond waters at night that invited increased submarine activity. In either case, tension and discomfort were pervasive. For the first two-and-a-half years of the sea war, Canadian sailors in most instances went into battle with less training than their counterparts in the Royal Navy. They were forced to use antiquated equipment such as the notoriously primitive radar set called the SWIC whose complex aerial was called a "yagi," apparently named for a Japanese physicist who had something to do with its development, but hardly reassuring, said Lamb, because "everyone knew whose side *he* was on."[7] Rushed through training, sent to sea with museum-pieces for equipment, and led by inexperienced skippers, the crews faced inevitable disaster.

In September 1941, Canadian escorts were boiling across the Atlantic, shepherding sixty-four merchant ships in convoy No. SC-42. Ironically, above the flotilla, Mackenzie King was aboard the Liberator bomber that was now returning him to Canada from his trip to England. At some point, they certainly crossed paths, King munching sandwiches, sipping soup and dozing on his divan at 10,000 feet, while below a hastily assembled group of Canadian escorts plunged through a gale. They included HMCS *Skeena*, a destroyer, and corvettes *Alberni*, *Kenogami* and *Orillia*. Later, *Chambly* and *Moose Jaw* caught up with the main force.

On September 10, the convoy was attacked by a wolf pack of at least eleven U-boats. The hit-and-run battle stretched over several days, a cacophonous shoot-out reminiscent of a wild-west movie. When it ended, the German submariners counted sixteen merchant ships as their victims. While the Canadian escorts managed to send one U-boat to the bottom (the first of the war), the battle was disastrous for the Canadians. There were near-collisions with the merchantmen they were protecting, questionable leadership, and sometimes utter confusion. At one point, one of the corvettes hove-to, removing itself from attack to pick up survivors from a doomed freighter. *Skeena* had no radar or high-frequency direction-finding equipment, and the destroyer had no or little experience in U-boat hunting; *Kenogami* was manned by a green crew and her skipper was on his first war patrol. *Moose Jaw* had gone to sea without full provisions, and her captain reported most of the crew was incapacitated by sea-sickness. Although there were mitigating circumstances, the result was still nothing less than disaster.

The following year was worse. One after another, Canadian-escorted convoys suffered grim losses: in August 1942, convoy SC-107 was attacked by sixteen U-boats, losing a third of her merchant ships, fifteen out of forty-two, to be precise. Despite their rakish élan, the Canadians were no match for the more experienced German wolf packs. Part of the problem, besides inadequate equipment, was the hard fact that there simply were not enough properly trained crews. By the end of 1942, the RCN now counted a war fleet of 200 fighting ships. In order to man them, the navy was cannibalizing sea-going ships of their crews. Unfortunately, the make-shift strategy was a failure. As 1942 came to a close, Allied shipping losses amounted to a staggering 7,790,000 tons and represented 1,664 ships lost to the U-boats.

The RCN was living on borrowed time. A year before, one of its senior officers had decided that ''RCN corvettes have been given so little chance of becoming efficient that they are almost more of a liability than an asset,'' and added sarcastically, ''At present most escorts are equipped with one weapon of approximate precision — the ram.''[8] Despite the fact that the Canadians had borne the brunt of the U-boat attacks in the North Atlantic for the last six months of 1942, ''eighty per cent of all ships torpedoed in the Atlantic (in November and December) were hit while being escorted by Canadian groups."[9]

By the end of 1942, the Canadian escort groups were pulled from battle to be "cycled through a period of consolidation and training."[10]

King and the War Cabinet acquiesced to the Admiralty. There was nothing else to be done. An interesting question is whether the manpower shortages, caused by strained technical facilities, would have been significantly alleviated had conscription been enforced after the declaration of war. An even more crucial question was how conscripts would have performed in this life-and-death ocean combat if, that is, a proud navy would have accepted them in the first place.

Ironically, it was the sailors' war that affected Mackenzie King in a most personal and direct way. In late September 1943, the destroyer *St. Croix* had been torpedoed by a U-boat. Angus L. Macdonald, minister of national defence for naval services, pulled King aside and ominously said, "I have bad news for you." Macdonald then told King, "I'm afraid your nephew is among the number missing."[11] King's nephew was Surgeon Lieutenant Lyon King, RCNVR.

For the next three days, King was preoccupied with consoling the immediate family. He talked by telephone with Lyon's wife, Margery, who was taking the dreadful news stoically and bravely. "Her voice was very clear and very fine," King wrote.[12] In Denver, Colorado, the boy's mother told King she had had a premonition. "Willie," she said, "I have all this week felt something was wrong." Young Lyon was one of the twin sons of King's brother, Macdougall. By coincidence, the surviving twin, Arthur, was in Ottawa with his wife, Kathleen. Since no one had yet informed Arthur, the task fell to King, who only a few days previously had helped the young couple find an apartment in Ottawa. He invited Arthur and Kathleen to Laurier House for lunch, accompanied them on an inspection of their flat just down the street, and asked them back to his library for coffee. Not knowing exactly how to tell Arthur and his wife, King began by speaking of the war generally, mentioning in his discourse how the *St. Croix* had been torpedoed. When King mentioned the name of the ship, "tears came into Kay's eyes." Arthur, not as robust as Lyon, was disconsolate. For the next three days, King's diary was full of details of the sad event, and of thoughts about Lyon. "I thought of him often," King wrote. "How splendid he looked the last time I saw him, wearing the fine uniform of a Surgeon Lieutenant of the Navy." King, who believed everyone's fate was pre-determined, was not gripped with remorse. "He was doing his duty and seeking to do it in the fullest and bravest manner possible," King wrote, "and that is what really matters." While there was a slight hope there would be survivors, only one sailor was rescued. Oddly, if not perversely, King read much interpretation into Lyon's death at sea, thoughts that he put on paper and are worth examination:

> No single event of the war, thus far, stands out in connection with fighting of a lot of men on sea, on land and in the air more significantly than this particular battle of the convoy . . . and the loss of all but one that were aboard St. Croix. More and more I cannot resist feeling that in a mysterious way, it is a repaying by Lyon to me with his life, for what I have done in its course for him. His gift to me is, of course, to link me closer into that community of suffering of those who have lost their own in the war, and though it would be the last thing one would like to happen as a means of increasing political power on the part of a leader in the govt., it nevertheless inevitably will have that effect. In this mysterious way, God is working out his own purpose.

Even in tragedy, King could not seem to separate private grief from political advantages. In this case, the reader might have wished that King was not so candid in his most private thoughts.

By the spring of 1943, the Canadian escorts were back in battle, equipped with improved radar and direction-finding gear, followed the next year by faster frigates and improved corvettes. In 1944, the RCN got the newest depth charge launchers, enabling it to press the enemy back to the Irish Sea, the Bay of Biscay and the English Channel where during Operation Neptune and the invasion of Normandy, the RCN found itself in fierce battles where it acquitted itself with distinction. The amateur days of the early 1940s, fought aboard leaking rust buckets with dubious equipment, were over.

The Royal Canadian Navy lost twenty-four ships and close to two thousand officers and men during World War II, the lowest casualty rate of any of the Canadian fighting services. This, of course, seemed odd given the risks they faced. But the toll they extracted from the enemy was much worse. Germany lost a total of 632 U-boats, 47 of them sunk or captured by the RCN. Three out of every four U-boat sailors who put to sea didn't survive the war. More than 28,000 were killed between 1939 and 1945.

Mackenzie King never wavered in the face of the navy's many crises and never lost sight of the navy's role. In a War Committee meeting in May 1943, the subject of building a naval-air branch within the RCN was stoutly opposed by King. He felt it would be expensive and would shift direction from the navy's first and crucial task—escorting convoys. "I stressed the point," King told committee members, "that our navy's obligation was the lifeline between this continent and Britain."[13] That emphasis never changed, although in the process the navy became expert in anti-submarine warfare. After 1943, too, there developed a renewed ésprit de corps. Green maple leaves began appearing on ships' smoke-stacks; even without them, there was no mistaking Canadian identity. What other country could have named their ships *Haida*, *Huron* and *Athabaskan*, *Saguenay* and *Moose Jaw*, *Chicoutimi*, *La Pas* and *Wetaskiwin*? By the end of the war the RCN had grown to 775 ships of all kinds, and its ranks swelled to 107,000 men and women—the third largest navy in the allied cause. In the end, too, they looked like the sailors they had become, whether at action stations at sea or swinging off the back of a streetcar at Hamilton's King and James streets on shore leave—the youngest old sea-dogs in the world.

King, however, never devoted as much time to the navy as he did to the other branches of the services, especially the air force, which he had begun to promote and develop on the eve of war for purely ulterior motives.

CHAPTER NINE

The Airman's War

ONE DAY IN MAY 1976, Albert Speer, Hitler's personal architect and wartime minister of armaments, found himself with three Canadian film makers in the dining room of the comfortable Hotel Kempinski near Berlin's Kurfurstendamm. The Canadians had just completed the filming of a documentary profile on Speer and his role inside the Third Reich. Although the film shooting had stopped, the questions continued. Had there been one single event in the war that was significant in bringing down the Nazis, someone asked? Not really, Speer mused. There were simply too many factors and, in truth, they all combined to spell *finis*. However, allied air supremacy was a major factor contributing to the collapse with the unrelenting rain of bombs. When one of the film makers asked if Speer had been aware of the British Commonwealth Air Training Plan, Speer admitted with candour that he had not, and asked quizzically, ''Tell me about this?''[1]

Where to begin? In the late 1930s the RAF had expressed interest in establishing a training program for its pilots in Canada. The idea was given little credence in Ottawa during initial discussions simply because Mackenzie King found any scheme under British control on Canadian soil was a challenge to Canadian sovereignty. But shortly after war was declared, the idea was resurrected and talks began in earnest between Canada and a special British mission that had come to Ottawa, headed by Lord Riverdale, the U.K. industrialist. It soon was apparent that Riverdale was trying to railroad the Canadians into signing an agreement that wasn't much different from the earlier suggestion that Canada should allow the RAF carte blanche in training pilots and other air crew members. The smooth-tongued, rough-hewn Englishman doubted the RCAF's ability to mount such an undertaking, and felt that it best be left to the RAF. King adamantly refused, displaying instead negotiating skills that must have surprised the Britons, including the old mediator's trick of physically wearing down the other side. Reading between the lines of the official accounts of the negotiations, King's tactics were nothing short of browbeating the opponent; at one point King reminded Riverdale that he, Mackenzie King, "was speaking to him now as Prime Minister of Canada."[2] King also exerted pressure on Lord Tweedsmuir, then governor-general, to get Riverdale's signature on the document. This Tweedsmuir did, even though he was ailing and bedridden in Government House. When King was ushered into Tweedsmuir's sick-room, he found the governor-general frail and propped up on his pillows. King writes, "I had come on the most important matter I had ever had occasion to speak to him of." Up until that point of the war, it was.

Besides being a patriotic duty, King saw the formation of the training plan as having "clear political advantages."[3] Deeply embedded in King's mind was the horrible memory of the staggering losses Canada had suffered on the battlefields of the Great War. Passchendaele, the Somme and Vimy were names from the past that were synonymous with the slaughter of men in the trenches, events that eventually led to World War I conscription in Canada. For that reason alone "King was reluctant to see Canada committed to a major contribution of soldiers; he feared that casualties might be as great or greater in a second European war."[4] In the end, this goal was not achieved but there was no way that King or anyone else suspected otherwise that

December day in 1939 when the British Commonwealth Air Training Plan was signed and sealed.

The scheme was colossal in size, priced at an astonishing $1,281,000,000. Canada had never seen anything like it before and rarely since, rivalling construction of the Seaway, Canadian Olympic games' facilities or any big city subway system. The only undertaking since to have surpassed it was Quebec's gigantic James Bay power development of the 1970s. King had undertaken to build in a matter of months a hundred training airstrips from one end of Canada to the other, each self-sufficient with its own infrastructure of administration and operating facilities. It was a task that required the immediate formation of an industrial force. Superlatives pale in attempting to define the breadth of this massive construction challenge facing Canada in the winter of 1939–40. One and three-quarter million blueprints were produced for contractors charged with erecting 8,300 buildings, hangars, offices, billets, fire and drill halls, fuel storage tanks and latrines. The plan would initially need over 3,500 aircraft, a fleet so large it dwarfs all the combined fleets of all of today's passenger-carrying Canadian airlines. It would also need thousands of vehicles including snow-ploughs, tractors to pull the aircraft, fire trucks, and passenger cars and buses to transport the recruits. Equipment to be procured included everything from cannibal-size cooking vats to thousands of urinals and millions of light bulbs, not to mention tens of thousands of uniforms to clothe the trainees.

The sheer logistics were overwhelming, and given the urgency of the war situation, everything had to be done by yesterday. Each station was expected to be completed within six months of the first surveyor's stake being hammered into the ground. Naturally enough, given the haste involved, there were set-backs. The buildings were all pre-fabricated from wood, since steel was needed for war materials such as bombs, tanks and ships. The hangars averaged 224' × 160' in size and were made exclusively of wood; B.C. fir was used for the rafters, which were bolted together. In many instance, the wood was green and the hangars soon began to shrink. For years afterward, the buildings emitted a soulful moan accompanied by alarming cries of creaking wood, matching the protestations of a schooner at sea during a gale.

The first recruits, who began arriving in April 1940, often found conditions trying. At one station because of a bureaucratic foul up, the student-trainees lived on a steady diet of stewed tomatoes. At another airfield, the entire station complement came down with diarrhoea brought on by drinking water from newly installed pipes containing white lead. Worse, because the latrines had not yet been installed, the afflicted students found themselves negotiating open slit trenches, balancing themselves on undressed, splintery 2 × 4's. At Estevan, Saskatchewan, an urgent call went out for a steamroller. One was found nearby but it took the driver a week to reach the station since the machine travelled at only four miles an hour. When the taps were turned on at a station outside Dunville, Ontario, black water gushed into the basins. The recruits solved the problem by shaving and brushing their teeth with milk. Frequently trainees arrived before the stations were completed, so operators were forced to improvise. When installation of landing lights fell behind schedule at one station, workers filled tea-kettles with goose grease, which when set to the torch served as tiny beacons in the night along the length of the runways. Tools were often scarce as well. At a station in Quebec, mechanics used a store-bought tobacco cutter, usually used to cut tobacco for "makings," but in this instance fashioned to cut gaskets for airplane engines.

The air force had so few permanent professionals, civilian flying club members were contracted to teach elementary flying. Because no one had thought about how these instructors were to dress, there quickly appeared what everyone called a "prairie admiral's uniform"—a cross between a milkman and the doorman you might expect to see outside the Royal York in Toronto or the Hotel Windsor in Montreal. It seemed ironic that some of the instructors looked like milkmen; a lot of them were rough-and-tumble ex-bush pilots who drank their whisky neat.

In the beginning, the operation was almost an entirely Rube Goldberg affair of hit-and-miss and trial-and-error. To make it work required the imagination of a Cecil B. De Mille directing an extravaganza and the ruthlessness of an industrial magnate like Howard Hughes.

For the former, King found such attributes in Chubby Power, and for the latter, C.D. Howe, the minister of munitions and supply, a

man seen by his political opponents as the dictatorial, hard-fisted cap-
italist that Hollywood liked to depict in the movies of the 1930s.

Howe was impatient and sometimes testy, a man who startled friend
and foe alike with "his blunt talk" that was "uninhibited by diplomatic
niceties."[5] Once during debate in the House of Commons, Howe, in
replying to a member, said, "A cut of one million dollars in a war
appropriation would not be a serious matter." The remark got whittled
down in time and Howe got stuck with the famous phrase, "What's
a million?" George Drew called Howe "a virtual dictator" because
of the power he wielded from his post in supply and munitions. Another
member called him "a fascist . . . but a nice fascist."

Clarence Decatur Howe was American-born, a New England Yan-
kee, who surfaced as a professor of civil engineering at Dalhousie
University in Halifax in 1908. When the academic life became too
tame for Howe, he struck out on his own. By the time he had come
into King's Cabinet in 1935 as the member from Port Arthur, Howe
had made millions in engineering and construction and was considered
a world expert in building grain elevators. His first cabinet post was
as minister of transport and it was this department that established the
Crown-owned Trans-Canada Airlines. In April 1940, Howe also took
on the portfolio of minister of munitions and supply, about the time
the country was breaking ground and letting contracts for the lands,
buildings and equipment needed to get the air training plan off the
ground. Fortuitously for King, although Howe and the prime minister
often differed sharply on many issues, there was no one else so
obviously qualified as the crusty "C.D.", as he became known; he
was a man who had spent his life building bridges, docks, factories
and a national airline.

Among his many duties was acting as the supervising minister of
the War Supply Board which, given broad powers by an order-in-
council under the War Measures Act, operated with unaccustomed
freedom from red tape and profit restrictions. One of Howe's first
decisions was to bring into the government's war effort many of the
nation's so-called captains of industry, such as Wallace Campbell,
president of the Ford Motor Company. In Ottawa's power circles these
movers and shakers became known as the "dollar-a-year-men."

Howe was equally direct with the men he hired. When Ralph Bell, the head of a Halifax fishing and shipping firm, was asked by Howe to take charge of the country's new aircraft production program, Bell replied that while he held a private pilot's licence he didn't know anything about building aircraft. According to co-biographers, Robert Bothwell and William Kilbourn, Howe snapped back, "I didn't ask you that. I said I wanted you to take charge."[6] Bell did just that.

Almost a month to the day after taking over the newly created ministry of munitions and supply, Hitler's armies were rolling through Luxembourg and the Lowlands, toppling the countries like bowling pins in a startling new method of warfare — Lightning War or Blitzkrieg. Holland crumbled in a mere four days, Belgium in sixteen. By the end of May, German panzers had driven the British army on to the beaches at Dunkirk on the English Channel where it barely, yet miraculously, escaped capture. A remarkable evacuation plan involved a hastily gathered fleet comprising everything from destroyers to Thames River yachts, manned by Sunday sailors displaying indomitable spirit. Everyone called the evacuation at Dunkirk a miracle. To Howe it was a disaster. It meant the first shipment of British aircraft that were to be supplied for training in Canada was suddenly put on hold in England. With the Nazi army sitting twenty-odd miles across the Channel, the threat of invasion was chillingly real. Every and any piece of military equipment, training aircraft notwithstanding, might be needed in a battle to push back the enemy. Canada had been counting on receiving 1,500 twin-engine Ansons to complete the training of bomber crews.

Undaunted by the set-back, Howe immediately set up a government-owned corporation to co-ordinate building the airframes for the Anson. The company was called Federal Aircraft. Howe got the engines for the planes from a manufacturer in, of all places, Pottstown, Pennsylvania. The problem was that the engines and instruments were American, the airframe design British, and Federal Aircraft was a company with no experience in the aviation field. Soon there were problems. When production lagged, Howe came under vicious attack in the Commons; the millionaire with the bushy eyebrows and granite

chin carried the battle alone with only a few brief interjections of
support from King.

In the heat of battle, Howe snapped at his critics, "If any of them
want my job, they are welcome to it."[7] His arrogance was matched
only by his managerial skills. "In the end," said Leslie Roberts, one
of Howe's biographers, "the best answer to the Anson debate lay in
the results achieved. By June 1, 1943, 1,850 Canadian-built Ansons
were flying, or 350 more than the initial target of 1,500. Canada had
in that time also produced 2,360 elementary trainers at DeHavilland
and Fleet Aircraft, and 3,578 advanced training machines. In addition
Canada had turned out 2,076 service aircraft; a grand total of 8,014
from an industry which had been virtually non-existent before the war."
Howe's style was never better illustrated than at an airplane christening
when he gruffly told the dignitary swinging the bottle of champagne,
"Will you christen this plane and let us get back to our jobs?"

King's appointment of Howe attested to his unmatched talent for
picking the right person for the job, which he also demonstrated when
he appointed Chubby Power as minister for air in July 1940. Although
King fretted over Power's continued drinking, he recognized Power's
obvious leadership skills which got results, such as defeating Duplessis
only the year before.

Power's style was considerably different from Howe's. His easy
charm disguised a decisive mind. When Power took over the department, he discovered its high-ranking members thought the "Minister
was little more than a mouthpiece to express in Parliament the views
and opinions of the members of the Air Council."[8] Power stunned the
brass by firing one of the top men, Air Vice Marshal G.M. Croil,
whom he found too regimented and hidebound. Moreover, Power
sensed there was a "degree of antipathy between the uniformed members of the forces and the numerous civilian staff. I felt that Croil's
influence would lean altogether too heavily on the side of the uniform
and so would upset the balance." In short order, Croil was sent packing
overseas. Despite the fact that Power lacked even the most elementary
comprehension of the vastness and extent of the Air Training Plan,
and that he "knew nothing of mechanics or engineering," he ran the
operation with aplomb, as was shown when an underling complained

that bureaucracy was causing a shortage of Air Force greatcoats. Power promoted the man and put him in charge of the bureaucracy so as to unplug the pipeline. He did.

Power also saw the value of public relations. If he lacked the ability to understand the vastness of the Air Training Plan himself, what did the average Canadian know? Power hired members of the advertising and public relations staff of the huge Massey-Harris farm equipment manufacturers to sell the project, and talked Billy Bishop, VC, the World War I flying hero, into taking to the rubber-chicken circuit to promote the scheme. This was a likely partnership because Bishop, like Power, was a prodigious drinker, a charming talker who cut a dashing figure in his Air Marshal's uniform, and a man who "gargled with gin in the morning."[9]

The early success of the Air Training Plan was clearly evident in the numbers of men it began graduating. By 1942, nearly 24,000 aircrew had gone through the system, half of them being posted directly overseas to RCAF and RAF squadrons; the latter became a considerable irritant in the scheme of things. There arose a cry from within the Air Force and, to some extent, from the public for fuller representation of Canada as a nation in the air war. The growing controversy was brought to a head when the Air Officer Commanding-in-Chief of the RCAF overseas sounded off in an interview that was widely carried in Canadian papers. Although Harold "Gus" Edwards was an Air Vice Marshal, he talked like a Hollywood tough guy. Edwards described the critics of the so-called "Canadianization" of the RCAF, who thought it might split the Empire, as nothing but a bunch of "mugs."[10]

The problems were complex, ranging from the kind of shoulder patches the Canadians wore, to pay and benefits to an extremely complicated financial debt that Canada was trying to foist on Britain, since Britain had failed to deliver many of the training planes in the original agreement. Power was candid enough to confess that all the financial conditions involved in the matter of air training left him confused. So, like any good manager, he hired more experts to solve the growing dilemma, in this instance, the august talent of a partner in the Montreal accounting firm, Price, Waterhouse and Co. Power eventually solved many of the problems revolving around how commissions were granted, promotion, tours of duty, and home leave. But "Canadianization" of the RCAF was never fully realized, although many purely Canadian squadrons were formed along with a fully Canadian manned bomber group.

Despite the frenzied haste surrounding the training of the aircrew (many trainees went solo in just eight hours), and makeshift procedures, the British Commonwealth Air Training Plan became a decisive factor in the air front over Germany. The BCATP graduated 131,553 pilots, bomb aimers, navigators and wireless operators and supplied forty-five per cent of all Commonwealth squadrons. There is no doubt whatsoever that the plan was "a major contributor to the air supremacy Allies achieved in every theatre of the war by 1944."[11] The RCAF sent 72,835 recruits through the system and with parallel training had itself grown from a pre-war complement of several hundreds to nearly a quarter of a million men and women by war's end. "And that," said one of the Canadian film makers to Albert Speer in the dining room of the Hotel Kempinski in Berlin, "was the British Commonwealth Air Training Plan."[12] The old Nazi seemed impressed.*

The Canadian airman's war was in fact particularly gruesome, both for himself and the enemy upon whom his wrath fell. How Mackenzie King, on the eve of war, could have thought otherwise is puzzling. In World War I, a scant fifteen years after the birth of aviation, it had become apparent just what the impact of the air weapon was going to be in future wars. Even then, Canadians had been in the forefront in the development of this startling and new form of warfare. Canadians in the 1914–18 war made up most of the squadron personnel of the Royal Flying Corps that launched the first bombing raids against

---

*Dining that night in Berlin with Speer were the author, Patrick Watson and William R. Cunningham, at that time the vice-president of News, of the *Global Television Network*, which had comissioned the documentary on Speer.

German cities. Yet nothing matched in significance the role Canadians came to play twenty-two years later in the RAF's Bomber Command, which "produced a scale of devastation in the cities and towns of Germany and of other European countries wildly beyond any prewar conception of what a modern bomber force could achieve."[13]

Of course, war knows no ethics or morality. To paraphrase George Orwell, if the enemy drops one bomb on your mother, you drop two on his mother. It was certainly an attitude King shared and there is no evidence to suggest otherwise. His foresight in establishing the air training program and his talent in assigning perfect managers to direct it was quite remarkable, matched only by a complete and totally clinical detachment when faced with the results of its depth of destruction. The raid on Dresden was an example.

One night in mid-February 1945, two waves of Lancaster bombers totalling 1,325 aircraft, including 70 Canadian machines, dropped 2,500 tons of high-explosive and incendiary bombs on the sleeping city. The result was nothing less than fearful. The numerous fires started by the incendiary bombs began competing with each other for oxygen, creating one gigantic ball of fire, or firestorm, that sucked every cubic inch of air out of every building or shelter. Those who weren't burned to death suffocated by inhaling the carbon monoxide created by the flames. At least 40,000 died, although some figures place the toll at more than 50,000. Both Berlin and Hamburg had suffered similar raids, though not with the same grim results that were Dresden's.

King's reaction when he learned of the terrible raid was strangely dispassionate. On March 5, King mentioned Dresden in his diary but in a context that was more related to bricks and mortar than human lives. "The war situation, too, is most promising, though terribly sad," King wrote, ". . . Berlin, Dresden, Cologne—all beautiful cities— pretty much completely destroyed."[14] There was no mention of the loss of life.

In truth, King's attention was focused on Canadian casualties. The RCAF's casualties were disturbingly high. (The RCAF's death toll exceeded 17,000 killed in all theatres of operations.) Yet, for the prime minister, the high casualty rate was not politically disastrous.

Young Canadians, despite the savagery of the air war, continued to line up to volunteer in the air force and did so to the very end of the war. For the prime minister, their patriotic courage averted any possible crisis of a need for replacements.

This was not the case for the army. In the summer of 1944 the casualty lists in the army grew alarmingly, as did Mackenzie King's worst fears at the prospect of having to impose conscription.

CHAPTER TEN

The Soldier's War

O F ALL THE LEADERS of the western Allies, Mackenzie King was the least military figure in either appearance or experience. He had never flown in a military aircraft (let alone any kind of airplane) until after the war began. King was a terrible sailor, frequently seasick on his many ocean voyages. Unlike Churchill, who served as a lieutenant-colonel on the Western Front in 1916, or Roosevelt, who was for seven years the assistant secretary of the navy, King was a neophyte in military matters. Despite his shortcomings, King balanced his leadership with astute and flawless judgement in picking the men who were to direct the fortunes of Canada's army, navy and air force. Chubby Power's political savvy and entrepreneurial skills made him a competent and effective minister for air. Angus L. Macdonald, the former premier of Nova Scotia, was a compassionate and decisive minister of national defence for naval services. When Norman Rogers was killed in an airplane crash, King's appointment of J.L. Ralston to the country's critical post of minister of national defence was nothing less than inspired. Although King would have a falling out with all three, he wisely and rarely interfered with their daily decisions. But when he did it was because King's antennae detected potentially dangerous political repercussions. But of all the fighting services, it was the army and its rapid expansion that King followed most closely. Remembering the fearful casualties that the Canadian army suffered in World War I, King was dedicated to preventing a repetition of history.

When war came in 1939, Canada's standing army of a mere 4,500 troops was woefully ill-equipped. Their arms were of the 1914–18 vintage, horses were still being used in some units as late as the 1930s, and there were not enough steel helmets for every man. Even so, it was a remarkable achievement when Canada was able to send the 1st Division to England by December 1939, made up of members of the tiny permanent force and troops from the non-permanent active militia units. All volunteered to go overseas. But after June 1940, when the National Resources Mobilization Act (NRMA) was passed, Canada in effect created two armies.

While every male over the age of sixteen was required to register for national service, only volunteers were accepted for overseas service. Those who voluntarily enlisted, or decided "to go active," became known as "General Service" men. The compulsorily enlisted were referred to as "NRMA" men. They could not be sent abroad.

As the war dragged on, the ranks of the non-volunteers grew steadily. By November 1944, their numbers were close to 60,000 and had become the object of derision by the fighting troops and the target of scorn by most of the civilian population outside of Quebec. There was little doubt that the NRMA men were genuinely despised. Canadians called them "Zombies" for their apathetic refusal to fight. They were frequently harassed by their NCOs, set upon by vigilante patriots, and spurned at dances by women whose menfolk had enlisted by choice. It was unfair, of course, to call all the NRMA men quivering cowards. This home defence army, as it was also called, was made up of men who were either too young or too old to fight; others were medically unfit for combat or served as tradesmen. While 58,348 Zombies eventually decided to volunteer for active service, an almost equal number nevertheless stood fast in the face of growing indignation and created a phantom army. By 1944, the Zombies came to haunt Mackenzie King more threateningly than any of the private ghosts ever had.

During the first three years of the war, to King's immense relief, there were minimal Canadian land casualties, excluding the disaster at Hong Kong. And it was only luck that prevented similar results in France in 1940 following the British evacuation of Dunkirk. In a bone-headed military undertaking of which little has been written, units of the 1st Canadian Division were sent to France where they found themselves hurtling inland amidst confusion and near chaos, toward Laval and Le Mans. But days after landing on July 12, the Germans entered Paris and the Canadians began a hasty retreat to Brest. Other units escaped by a speeding train to the port of St. Malo. Luckily, a British transport ship was tied up at St. Malo and the Canadians safely sailed for Southampton. They had come close to tasting disaster. Extraordinary luck saved them but in the mad dash across the French countryside, the Canadians lost most of their equipment: some personal weapons, and about 216 cars, trucks and gun carriers. Remarkably, only one soldier was killed (in a road accident) and only a handful were captured.

That was not the case two years later in August 1942, when 5,000 Canadians stormed the small French sea-coast town of Dieppe. It was not so much a battle as a complete slaughter. If the Brest excursion had been militarily dumb, Dieppe was criminal. The latter-day visitor to the town—called the poor man's Monte Carlo because of its lone gambling casino — merely has to stand on the towering cliffs overlooking the stony beach to realize the futility of the assault. No Canadian engagement has been so thoroughly examined. And deservedly so, because of the incompetence of its planners, from Lord Louis Mountbatten, the chief of combined operations, to Harry Crerar, who was appointed by General McNaughton as "the responsible military officer"[1] for Operation Jubilee (as the Dieppe raid was called). At the time, McNaughton was the senior officer of the Canadian Army Overseas. At one planning session before the raid, Crerar was challenged by Trafford Leigh-Mallory, Air Vice-Marshal, who headed the RAF's No. 11 Group of Fighter Command. Leigh-Mallory told Crerar: "Your plan may have merit in theory, but it's damned impracticable. The troops will be pinned down on the beaches at the very beginning. They'll never get going again, you mark my words.'' This was exactly what happened. Years later, Crerar tried dodging responsibility, as he had done over the debacle at Hong Kong, by saying the Dieppe raid was "basically a British plan." Terence Robertson, author of *The Shame and the Glory — Dieppe*, concluded that both Crerar and McNaughton "possessed ultimate military authority and apparently did little to alter the planning." This was a clear indication that both Canadian generals must have concurred with the principal features of the Dieppe raid.

As the horrible facts emerged from the August 19, 1942, raid, Mackenzie King correctly assessed the disaster. "I still have a feeling," he wrote, "that the part of wisdom would have been to conserve that especially trained life for the decisive moment. It may, in the long run, prove to be for the best but such is war. It makes me sad at heart."[2] Conventional wisdom has since confirmed King's instincts, that the lessons learned that awful summer day at Dieppe paid dividends later when the Allies launched the Normandy invasion two years later. That assessment was little solace to the wives, mothers, brothers and sisters of the 5,100 Canadians who took part. Three-quarters of them were killed, wounded or taken prisoner, all within six hours. Even so, Mountbatten never recanted. "If I had the same decision to make again," he said, "I would do as I did before."[3]

While the Canadian soldier's defeat at Dieppe was a spectacular failure, he showed himself as a tough, individual fighter. And by the time of the invasion of Sicily on July 10, 1943, Canadian soldiers had become some of the best-trained troops in the Allied forces. At that time, thousands of Canadians had already been in the overseas army for two-and-a-half years. Moreover, they were superbly fit. The only thing the Canadian lacked was battle experience, and as he advanced across the Sicilian toe of the Italian boot and on up the spine of the country, he quickly became seasoned. The same could be said of the Canadian troops in the Normandy campaign in the summer of 1944, although many were green troops.

In many ways, the Canadian infantryman, tank trooper and artilleryman was a unique fellow. He made up an army of civilians that was led by officers who had come through the ranks of pre-war militia units. There were in fact few professional soldiers. In both cases all had volunteered to fight overseas. Yet no amount of training could match experience in battle and despite the most technological war ever to be fought, it was still the ground soldier who won or lost the seemingly endless battles, frequently at the closest of quarters and with the most primal instincts. The soldier's war was a contest more tactile than scientific—a caveman's fight. Compared to the air force or navy's often remote and clinical execution of the enemy, the soldier's war was akin to fighting and killing with rocks and clubs, skills that had to be learned in the harshest classroom of them all—the battlefield.

Who were these students of battle? In all respects, unremarkably ordinary. In 1942, a profile of the Canadian soldier took shape after the army gathered statistical data on the fighting soldier. In the first instance, he was less educated than his counterpart volunteers in the air force or navy. Only two per cent had finished Grade 6. His average age was 19½ years. He came from every walk of life. "About a quarter had lived on farms, another quarter came from towns of 4,000 people or less, another quarter had lived in towns and cities with a population between 4,000 and 80,000, while the remainder came from large cities of 80,000 and over."[4] To survive, the Canadian soldier had to adapt to the toughest conditions, considerably worse than those experienced by sailors and airmen. Once in battle, the soldier lived almost exclusively in the open, in the severest weather. In the line, he slept in a hole in the ground that he himself dug — what the army called slit trenches. Curiously, this primitive lair was almost completely safe and effective from enemy fire except for a direct hit. Going into battle he carried a shovel, his weapon, magazine clips of ammunition and his "tin" hat; for food he packed a monotonous diet of canned bully beef, biscuits or hardtack and chocolate. He drank tea, often heavily laced with rum which his NCOs liberally distributed. The weather was as debilitating as the enemy. It was debatable whether the hammering heat of an Italian summer was worse than the penetrating cold and demoralizing rain of a French or Dutch winter. In those climes, the soldier layered himself in long johns, wool shirts and sweaters under his shapeless woollen battle jacket. He wore a toque under his helmet

and carried extra socks. He recycled discarded wet socks by placing
them around his waist where his body heat would dry them. Nothing,
absolutely nothing, was worse than wet feet. Nearly everyone smoked,
incessantly. Even given today's abundance of information on the deadly
effects of tobacco, such news wouldn't have changed the soldier's
habit in the least. Out of the line, he craved a number of comforts:
uninterrupted sleep, a hot meal and bath, dry clothes, liquor and female
companionship, and it didn't matter in which order. Mail, too, was
important. The soldier too often drank himself senseless. Once out of
the battle line the soldier's kit bag usually caught up with him, which
meant a much needed change of clothes. Out of the line, too, his billet
could be anything from the floor of the men's room in an Italian railway
station to the vestry of an equally cold Belgian church. Although when
he had joined up, he had sworn allegiance to the King, his first allegiance was to himself and, next, to several close buddies, his squad,
platoon, company, battalion and regiment, probably in that order. In
battle, the Canadian soldier was magnanimous to his fellows who
cracked under the tension of this life and death struggle. He was less
generous with anyone who imperilled his tenuous existence by careless
movement that would reveal the unit's presence to the enemy, and
thereby draw fire. Contrary to fiction and film in which enlisted men
hated officers, the Canadian soldier respected his officers, especially
so if they were experienced in combat. A wise, experienced and cautious officer kept his men alive. He was wary of new officers. The
last kind of officer he wanted was the Errol Flynn type leaping over
the parapet. All these attitudes and skills were acquired only by experience, a process that took considerable time. When fresh replacements
arrived, they were quickly adopted and slowly taught the ropes. This
way everyone's longevity was extended. Although the Canadian soldier
was not highly educated, he became as observant as a landscape painter
studying distant hills, as skilled as a land surveyor in assessing the
contours of the land, and as resourceful as a farmer living on some
isolated homestead far from civilization. He also learned the critical
art of concealment. He learned how to hold his breath when poking
his head above the rise that hid him from the enemy's eyes. He knew

that even the merest hint of condensation from his breathing might be the difference between life and death.

It was a curious fact, too, that no one occupation in civilian life was more suitable than another for this role of a soldier in battle. The great high-school athlete was no better suited to the battlefield than the farm kid, or the undernourished teenager from a city slum. They all looked the same in the enemy's gunsight whether it be rifle, mortar or artillery. What made a soldier effective was the slow task of learning the fundamental rules of combat, not the least being the acquired ability to balance fear; although some of his fellows displayed inexplicable fearlessness, most of the soldiers had to learn the lessons that would assuage the constant threat of death. They were simple lessons: for instance, knowing the difference between the sound of the enemy's Spandau and his own Vickers, and the closeness of an incoming high explosive artillery shell. All this knowledge was of incalculable value, but each lesson learned grew more costly as the war progressed. On June 6, 1944, the focus of the war shifted to the beaches of Normandy, where other Canadians, new to battle, began to learn the process all over again. It was an incredible summer when the fate of Europe hung in the balance, as did Mackenzie King's own future as Canadian casualty figures began to mount, creating what C.P. Stacey called "one of the most violent and bitter public controversies in Canadian political history."[5] In the euphoria of victory, with Paris liberated and the once invincible German armies shattered and bloodied, it seemed to Mackenzie King nothing short of perversity that his leadership, judgement and veracity were now challenged at the very eleventh hour of battle. The date was Tuesday, September 19, 1944. That was the day the *Globe and Mail* of Toronto published a stunning accusation that the Canadian fighting divisions were being bled to death on the European battlefields because of a lack of replacements. Further, many of the reinforcements were so badly trained that sending them into battle was nothing short of murder. Worse for King was that the accuser was himself a brave soldier, terribly wounded and just back from the front. Canadians believed what they read. Connie Smythe, holder of the Military Cross, sportsman, family man, and founder of the Maple Leafs hockey dynasty, was someone who never pulled his punches.

PART IV

THE FINAL CRISIS
September 1944–
December 1944

CHAPTER ELEVEN

The Desperate Summer

HIS FAMILY REGISTERED HIS birth with the names Constantine Falkland Cary Smythe, but when his mother died in 1906 the boy, at his own insistence, called himself Conn. When he was just seventeen, he was homesteading in Northern Ontario, but a forest fire wiped him out in 1912. He soon returned to Toronto, where he enrolled at the University of Toronto in civil engineering. He played varsity football and hockey and hung around race-tracks. When World War I broke out Conn Smythe, at age nineteen, joined the army. By 1917 he had won a Military Cross for bravery in the field at Arras in France. Later, he joined the Royal Flying Corps and was shot down and wounded over no man's land. Captured by the Germans, Connie Smythe spent the next fourteen months as a prisoner-of-war. After being repatriated to Canada in 1919, he returned to university and later bought a sand and gravel pit and a dilapidated dump truck. Even though his business was flourishing and demanding much of his time, Smythe kept his hand in hockey matters. By the middle of the Depression, Smythe had turned the old Toronto St. Pats into the Toronto Maple Leafs and had built a new arena for the team to play in.

He could not be called by any stretch of the imagination a "nice guy." Driven by ambition, Smythe was tough, crude and direct. He was also somewhat of a minor bigot, showing a dislike for Roman Catholics. In business he was motivated by profit and achievement. In public, he remained a steadfast patriot. When World War II began, Smythe went back into the army as an artillery commander. Remarkably, in his fiftieth year, Smythe was back on the battlefield. On the night of July 25, 1944, Smythe was sitting in a house near the banks of the Orne River in the suburbs of Caen when the Luftwaffe attacked. Running outside to help his men move a truckload of ammunition to safer ground, Smythe was critically wounded by a bomb blast. Evacuated to England, he began a painful convalescence and underwent an even more painful discovery: the reasons for mounting casualties in the ranks of the Canadian Army.

From the time Smythe was carried from the clearing station in Normandy, he began questioning other wounded officers about why they thought casualties were so high. A major from Les Fusiliers Mont-Royal, who had seen most of his unit killed or wounded, told Smythe that the replacements "were too green to go into battle without experienced non-coms leading them."[1] For the next two months, Smythe heard the same story repeated again and again. Worse, other wounded men told him how officers and men were being sent back into battle even before their wounds were properly healed. Smythe began documenting their stories, recording their names, serial numbers, units and the circumstances causing the high casualties. By the time he had been invalided home, Smythe's dossier was complete. When George McCullagh, publisher of the *Globe and Mail*, visited him at the Chorley Park military hospital in Toronto on September 18, the aging but combative Smythe was determined to go public with his findings. The next day the *Globe* printed his charges, which hit the public like a bomb blast. Accompanying the story was an editorial equally disturbing.

The reinforcement situation which he described in his statement will be a severe shock to many people, especially to the parents and families of our fighting men in Italy and France, and those who have relied on Defence Minister Ralston's repeated assurance that the Canadian Army had adequate reserves of trained reinforcements. . . . They come at a time when the Canadians are engaged in heavy fighting, casualties for which have not yet been reported. The implications are crystal clear to the least-informed citizen.[2]

The story and the editorial must have left readers confused. At that time, the Allies had long broken out of the Normandy bridgehead and Paris was back in the hands of the Allied armies. On September 4, the vital Belgian port of Antwerp had fallen to the British Second Army. Canadian forces were sweeping up the French coast liberating the Channel ports of Boulogne, Calais, Dunkirk, and most poignantly of all, Dieppe, where so many Canadians had fallen in the badly planned raid just two years before. Even as Canadians read Smythe's chilling accusation that large numbers of unnecessary casualties had resulted because reinforcements were "green, inexperienced and poorly trained,"[3] these same Canadian fighting men were already fighting to clear the enemy from the estuary of the Scheldt River that ran from the Port of Antwerp to the North Sea fifty-five miles away. Although Antwerp was in Allied hands, it was a useless possession as long as the Germans controlled both banks of the estuary. Until the enemy was driven back, no shipping dare run the river gauntlet from the open sea to the port. Barely a week after Smythe's accusations, the 2nd and 3rd Canadian Divisions and the 4th Canadian Armored Division had begun the drive to clear the estuary, a battle which in a few weeks became an epic struggle. Understandably, Canadians at home were perplexed. The Allied armies were rolling across France and into Belgium, and there was even talk that the war would end before Christmas.

It is interesting to read Mackenzie King's diary during this period. Few notations in the month of August relate to the fighting in Europe. In fact, in early August when George Drew, the Tory premier in Ontario, raised questions about the care of Canadian wounded, King penned a petulant attack against Drew in his diary for attempting to mar celebrations that were planned to mark King's twenty-fifth anniversary as leader of the Liberal party! "The whole thing clearly is deliberate," wrote King, "having as its objective not the matter of hospitalization, etc., which could have been brought up months ago or a week or days hence, but carefully related to just come on the 25th anniversary. This is typical Tory method. No sense of decency or chivalry."[4]

Perhaps even more revealing was an absence in his diary of any reaction to Smythe's charges. Weeks would pass before any such reference appeared. It was an entirely different reaction, however, that came from Defence Minister Ralston. Five days after Smythe made public his charges, Ralston left to visit the battle fronts himself. It's important to pause for a closer look at Ralston on the eve of his journey, for it would have a profound effect on both the physical and political life of Mackenzie King.

Of all King's wartime ministers, James Layton Ralston is perhaps the most difficult to put into focus. The prism of time has left us with a clouded image, not made clearer by his strange personality, including a peculiar dislike of people with blue eyes. "Whether he disliked them because of his experience with Mackenzie King, or he never fully trusted King because of his blue eyes, I never found out," remembered Walter Turnbull. "But, I thought a man in that position to have these little personal prejudices seemed to be a mark of great weakness, human if you like, but not the kind (of traits) which impartial statesmen are made."[5] There's no doubt that at the beginning of the war King thought highly of Ralston. However, animosity developed between them after King had moved Ralston from finance in July 1940, to succeed Norman Rogers as minister of national defence.

Ralston was born in Amherst, Nova Scotia, and like Chubby Power, had served in World War I. Ralston was a battalion commander and gained a reputation for bravery and competence. After the war he studied law and was called to the bar, an achievement which seemed not to entirely qualify Ralston in the eyes of at least one of King's mandarins. Years later, Jack Pickersgill remembered, "One of the great difficulties about Mr. Ralston, and it may seem kind of snobbery to say this, but I think he would have profited greatly from having gone to a university and not just to a law school. In the days when he became a lawyer, you didn't have to have an arts degree. He didn't have much capacity to detach himself from the day to day jobs."[6] Turnbull's memory of Ralston was similar. Ralston inevitably got caught up in the most minute administrative detail, immersing himself completely on the side of the team he was working for. Turnbull recalled that shortly after Ralston became minister of defence he began campaigning for increased funds for the services, "fighting with all his strength to get approved those things, which as Minister of Finance he'd fought hard to have turned down,"[7] mere hours before. "He would have been a very bad judge because Ralston was always the advocate." Ralston, who was always referred to simply as "the Colonel," was also a sentimental and compassionate man.

Grattan O'Leary recalled the night that his son, Owen, was reported missing in action. "It was a Sunday night and my wife and I were sitting at home; it was pouring rain and it was midnight. And my doorbell rang and I went to the door and there was Ralston, the Minister of Defence. He had left his office and came all the way to Rockcliffe to speak to me."[8] But, it was Ralston's excessive attention to detail that everyone mostly remembered. Years later, anyone who knew Ralston, even in the slightest, remarked on his fuss-budget personality. "He had," said O'Leary, "what Morley called 'a murderous tenacity about trifles!' " James Sinclair concurred: "This incredible attention for detail" certainly motivated Ralston to investigate first-hand the situation in Europe regarding casualty reports, "to almost count the troops himself."[9]

The night before his departure on September 24, Ralston met with King who inexplicably observed that his defence chief showed "the lightest heart that I think he has had for many a day."[10] That seemed a strange observation about a man who was embarking on a personal crusade to find out for himself exactly what truth there was in the reports of carnage on the battle front, which were now being raised daily in the press as a result of Connie Smythe's accusations. Smythe, incidentally, had since been informed by an officer who visited him in hospital that the army was going to court-martial him. Said Smythe, "You court-martial me and I'll publish every one of these names, the regiments they are with, the number of men they were short, when they went into battle, and what it cost in casualties.''[11] Then, the square-jawed tycoon told the army emissary to get out of his sight.

Connie Smythe never did face a court martial. He later claimed that Ralston himself ordered the army to drop the case against him because of the attendant publicity that a court martial would have generated. Besides, while there was no question of his insubordination, Smythe's accusations were true. Connie Smythe left the army shortly afterward.

Ralston arrived in Italy September 26 after an overnight stop in Gibraltar. Wearing his familiar homburg, he was an incongruous figure stomping the battle front, talking to both the brass and the troops. Ralston soon got an earful of woe. When he met Brigadier Eric Haldenby, commander of all the Canadian army holding units in Italy, Ralston was bluntly challenged: ''Do you want some figures to simply back up the government's stand, or do you want the truth?''[12] The truth was that all units were under-strength and worn out. In off-the-cuff interviews with regimental sergeant majors and NCOs, Ralston heard more horror stories about the lack of properly trained reinforcements. All of this was shortly confirmed by Major General Chris Vokes, who led the 1st Canadian Infantry Division. A top infantry commander, a graduate of both RMC and McGill, Vokes was somebody who didn't pussyfoot around. A substantial number of the replacements the army was receiving were under-trained, Vokes told Ralston. These were men who didn't have a chance to survive under fire, and to send them into action was ''an act of murder.''[13]

The situation in Italy was grim. At the time of Ralston's arrival, Canadians had been hard at fighting non-stop for close to fifteen months against a German army, who although in ordered retreat, had made the Canadians fight for every foot of the rugged Italian landscape. The Canadians had already penetrated three strong defence lines the Germans set up across the country's harsh interior; first there had been the Gustav Line, then the Hitler Line, and just the month before Ralton's visit, the Gothic Line. Casualties were nearing 18,000, with 2,836 dead. In fifteen months, the army had lost more men than the navy during the entire war. While everyone knew how capable the German army was with its lightning thrusts and mobility, Canadians suddenly came to realize the German soldier on defence was no less a formidable opponent. By the end of the summer of 1944, Canada and her Allies found this especially true in Normandy where Max Hastings proposed the Allies "faced the finest fighting army of the war, one of the greatest that the world has ever seen."[14] This was a simple truth, said Hastings, "that some soldiers and writers have been reluctant to acknowledge, partly for reasons of nationalistic pride, partly because it is a painful concession when the Wehrmacht and SS were fighting for one of the most obnoxious régimes of all time." Anyone who today visits the Canadian war graves of Normandy quickly understands the enormity of that struggle. By the end of August, Canadian casualties in France neared 10,000, a quarter of them dead.

By the end of his tour, James Layton Ralston was painfully aware of this sacrifice. Shaken, Ralston returned to London to confer with Lieutenant-General Kenneth Stuart, the chief of staff at Canadian Military Headquarters. Ralston's information, garnered at the front, differed from the facts being fed him from Stuart, who, only four months before D-Day, had undertaken the sole responsibility of informing the defence minister on the state of casualties and reinforcements. Stuart felt this procedure would spare Ralston from receiving conflicting and "alarmist cables."[15] In fact, on August 3, Stuart personally reported to the War Committee in Ottawa that all was fine on the battle front, and while some additional men were needed in Italy "we had plenty of reserves."[16]

However, on August 26, Stuart cabled Ralston the dramatic disclosure that there were not enough trained infantrymen to replace mounting casualties. Stuart then proposed that rear echelon troops, cooks, clerks and the like be temporarily shipped to the front line. Curiously, Ralston approved the recommendation without referring it to the War Committee. Denis and Shelagh Whitaker, in their gripping account of the battle of the Schedlt Estuary, *Tug of War: The Canadian Victory That Opened Antwerp*, wrote that "this was the first bare hint in Ottawa of the fact that untrained men were being sent into battle, but no one stirred in response."[17] Brigadier Whitaker, at that time a lieutenant-colonel, wrote in 1984 that every commander was well aware "of this travesty,"[18] — the ordering of untrained men into action. Although Whitaker, who after the war became a broadcaster and brewery executive, kept his silence for nearly forty years, his anger still raged when he publicly documented the colossal bungling that cost so many Canadian lives. Like the courageous soldier he was in battle, Whitaker's post-war attack on King was as direct as any of his wartime assaults. "The enemy," wrote Whitaker, "is not always on the other side of the hill."[19] To fighting soldiers like Whitaker and his comrades, Mackenzie King's pusillanimity was beyond contempt. Said one of Whitaker's company commanders, Joe Pigott, "We had only feelings of disgust, of contempt for the Prime Minister and the politicians who were not facing the realities of the crisis, and most of all, we felt anger. The feeling was becoming very deep-seated in all the troops that they were being used and being sacrificed by their government in order not to face public opinion."[20]

Another warrior, Ben Dunkelman, who also fought the Scheldt Estuary battle, was equally bitter. If Mackenzie King had somehow appeared in that battle area, "an unfortunate and unaccountable accident might have befallen his plump person," said Dunkelman.[21] While it goes without saying that the Canadian soldier had come to despise King, Whitaker's condemnation more directly focuses on Ralston's role in the crisis. Although Ralston began his personal tour to check firsthand if untrained Canadian replacements were being rushed into battle, it ended on the questioning note whether Canada had enough reinforcements of any kind. "About the standard of training," wrote Whitaker, "Ralston was silent. Whether he had persuaded himself that the men in front-line action were adequately trained—or was afraid that the world would discover they were not—he abandoned the investigation. In so doing, he abandoned the thousands of young untried Canadians flung into war with virtually no chance of survival."[22]

The confusion over Ralston's interpretation of the situation, at least as the Scheldt Estuary fighting was concerned, revolves around a meeting with Lieutenant-General Guy Simonds, commanding the First Canadian Army, and without doubt Canada's best fighting general of World War II. In any other country, Simonds certainly would have received the lionization he deserved, like a Patton or Rommel. In the eyes of Major-General Harry Foster, Simonds "was the brightest tactical army commander Canada had produced in any war."[23]

Analytical, decisive and indefatigable, Simonds was the "best we had," said Foster.

Yet, some historians claim Ralston came away from his meeting with Simonds believing that "taken as a whole, [the] standard of training of reinforcements is very satisfactory."[24] Whitaker, who was part of the battle, fiercely challenged historians on this point. The idea that Simonds told Ralston that his reinforcements were adequately trained "is an incredible statement to attribute to a man who had been deluged by reports to the contrary from all his staff." Whatever the case, as Ralston neared the end of his tour, he was in a state of deep depression, quite possibly triggered by a candid briefing by Field Marshal Montgomery himself. Montgomery told Ralston that after the Estuary was secured, the Canadians were then going to be assigned the task of clearing the west bank of the Rhine. Canadian casualties, said Montgomery, could most certainly expect to increase. The night before Ralston was scheduled to return to Ottawa, he dined with a handful of Canadian officers at Canadian headquarters in Antwerp. Those who attended discovered their guest almost totally silent, preoccupied and confused. One of the dinner guests was Richard S. Malone, a Winnipeg newspaperman who was serving as Canadian Liaison Officer to Montgomery. When dinner ended, Ralston invited Malone to join him in his trailer where he was to spend the night. Malone's description of Ralston is a moving one:

> There was a single light burning in the blacked out guest caravan and the only source of warmth was a small coal-oil heater which smoked away in one corner. To keep warm, I kept my trench coat on, but the Colonel appeared not to notice the cold and sat perched on the edge of the narrow bunk while we talked. It had been a long time since we had been able to talk quietly together and it was after three in the morning before I got on the road. The Colonel was terribly despondent and lonely. His mind was completely made up. . . . He would either force the government to bring in full conscription on his return or he would resign. For months before, the Colonel had been under almost continuous attack in the Canadian papers, which charged him with selling out on his own principles. They had dug up his conscription statements during the last war when he was serving as a battalion

commander in action. They claimed he was false to his own beliefs.

"I am not very popular at home now," the Colonel told me. I said I knew what was being said by the press and the public. But what appeared to concern the Colonel more was that he was at outs with some of his Cabinet colleagues. The one thought that was uppermost in the Colonel's mind all during the war was that units fighting overseas must have every support possible from home and not sent into action under strength or short of equipment. He would not let them down for political reasons now. He had been deeply moved by seeing hundreds of badly wounded men in field hospitals, men who had gone into action with regiments at half strength.

He had me draft a signal to send back to the Prime Minister, advising him of his return date to Ottawa and requesting "the earliest possible meeting with the Cabinet." Ralston stared at me silently for a moment. "King will know what that means," he said quietly.[25]

King most certainly did. Ralston's cable arrived on the afternoon of Friday, October 13, a superstitious day as everyone knows but which went unnoticed by King. The contents of the cable "occasioned me great concern," King wrote,[26] triggering in his mind the worst possible scenario for the future. "All this I can see means that he is coming back prepared to urge that the situation has become so much more serious than contemplated and that drastic steps will have to be taken to secure the necessary number of trained men." King spoke darkly of likely co-conspirators in the Cabinet, naming Angus Macdonald, and J.L. Ilsley, who had succeeded Ralston in finance. King huddled with St. Laurent, who confirmed King's suspicions that Ralston was about to destroy the Liberal government. St. Laurent said conscription must be opposed, agreeing with King that such action would create a Union government as happened during World War I when Sir Robert Borden returned from a similar overseas mission in 1917. As far as King was concerned any such development would dismember the British Empire and might even lead to annexation with the U.S. Just how this might lead to annexation King never explained. King pledged that none of these things "will take place under me." King also convinced himself that the days ahead were certain to be trying ones, all because Ralston was "a thorn in my flesh."

From that night on, and not until the end of the first week in December, would there be any respite for Mackenzie King. It was like some epic tragedy in which the leading players each night wrote the following day's lines, a convoluted plot so bizarre that Bruce Hutchison said it was "too fanciful even for fiction."[27] It was a story of deceit, betrayal and chicanery on the part of the leading actor, William Lyon Mackenzie King.

But as the political drama in Ottawa began to unfold, an even greater tragedy was taking place along the watery polders of Holland's Scheldt Estuary. There, Canadian soldiers found themselves fighting to the death in the war's worst battlefield. The land was flat as a billiard table, criss-crossed by dykes, rail lines and roads where the infantrymen were as exposed as if they were fighting on a flooded football field and being hammered by an enemy perched in the stands. All through the month of October, Canadians literally waded into battle, often waist deep in freezing water, clawing themselves inch by inch up the muddy slopes of the dykes and embankments, frequently fighting at such close quarters that battles were fought hand-to-hand with rifle butts and clubs.

It was from this battle front that Ralston took his leave to report to Prime Minister King. Early on the morning of October 18, 1944, Ralston, with General Stuart in tow, landed at Ottawa's Rockcliffe Airport. As the plane droned towards the capital, Mackenzie King was tossing and turning in a fitful sleep. Just before dawn, King had a vision. He saw himself shooting a gun at a bull's-eye, hitting the target four times out of five.

CHAPTER TWELVE

The Storm Bursts

ALSTON LOST NO TIME in reporting to Mackenzie King the desperate situation in Europe. They agreed to meet at King's office in the East Block at 5:00 P.M. the day Ralston returned. But, as King was leaving Laurier House, the defence minister suddenly appeared on his doorstep. Together, they drove to Parliament Hill. King observed that Ralston appeared to have aged dramatically and was suffering from a terrible head cold. The meeting began pleasantly enough in the Prime Minister's East Block Office. At first Ralston spoke in general terms; how it was now felt the war would last until spring, reporting the source of this information coming from no one less than General Montgomery, himself. Further, Ralston reviewed talks he had held with General Eisenhower, telling King that the Supreme Allied Commander confirmed Montgomery's view of hostilities lasting until the spring as well. Eisenhower said there would not be any cessation of fighting, no such thing as digging in for the winter, and that fighting would go on no matter what the weather might be. Then, Ralston shifted the conversation to the subject King feared most of all, the need to reinforce the hard-pressed Canadian fighting units, especially the infantry divisions that were taking the most serious losses. The storm of controversy that had been so long approaching now burst in full fury around Mackenzie King. The curtain of this drama over conscription slowly rose that autumn afternoon, and despite King's attempts over the past four years to delay, postpone, divert and avoid the question, there was no stopping James Layton Ralston from uttering the opening words. The details of the curtain raiser, and subsequent finale, were dutifully and, one suspects, accurately documented by King throughout the confrontation. To understand the events, even though they are doubtlessly coloured by King's own pen, his personal record still best evokes the flavour, tension and uncompromising positions of the leading players in the nation's greatest political drama of all time. For Mackenzie King it began this way:

> After a pause, Ralston said: Mr. King I want to speak of the question of reinforcements, which is a serious one. He went on to say that the fighting had been more intense than had been anticipated. Spoke of the numbers in the reserve being considerably less than had been anticipated when the estimate was made. This both in Italy and in Belgium and Holland; that the intensity and fighting had been greater and men had been kept longer in active conflict. He spoke particularly of some of the men who had been in Italy who had been away for five years and said that they would have to be allowed to come home. He then went on to say that he thought some of the men felt keenly about a standing army in Canada doing nothing while they were so short of reinforcements; that their morale for fighting would be increased if the reinforcements were larger. He spoke of visiting men in hospitals; seeing them go up to the front and others returning again to the fighting line. He did not wish to be emotional, but this had affected his feelings as to the necessity of easing the situation.[1]

Fully aware of Ralston's state of mind, King replied in a calm voice that to impose conscription at this stage of the war would only serve to confuse Canadians. Moreover, such a move would only create a repetition of what occurred in World War I when Borden returned from France and demanded conscription. It was a scar, said King, that still had not healed. He then spoke of the possible political consequences telling Ralston he "was perfectly indifferent" whether he remained in office, but that any move in the direction of conscription would certainly enhance the position of the C.C.F., and that he, Ralston, should fully understand this.[2]

As far as the military situation was concerned, King wondered whether it was reasonable, based on the facts at hand, that Germany was on its last legs. With France liberated and parts of Holland and Belgium in Allied hands, not to mention the advancing Red Army closing the ring from the east, how could one justify conscription at the eleventh hour? In any case, King continued, there would have to be a thorough discussion by a full cabinet to consider the matter. Ralston agreed and suggested he would prefer reporting to the War Committee first. King replied this would be arranged for the next day. Before Ralston left King, he apologized to the prime minister for adding "these burdens to others I have."[3] With those words, Ralston departed. He appeared to King to be a troubled, tired old man.

The prime minister decided to walk to Laurier House. The night was warm and he felt in need of fresh air. Jack Lay, King's chauffeur, had gone ahead to pick up Pat and to bring the pet to his master as he neared Laurier House. This was Pat No. 2, also an Irish terrier whom Joan Patteson had acquired for King following the death of the original Pat. As he strolled near the fire station on Laurier Avenue, King came upon a party of boys with whom he chatted, gaining a measure of comfort from his talk "with the little fellows."[4]

King inwardly admitted that if he had to rely on himself alone he might well despair. He took great comfort in the belief that it was Providence that guided and protected him. The strain was beginning to take its toll. For months, King had been troubled with ringing in his ears. He expressed alarm in his diary on that day that the ringing was at its worst ever. What he needed was complete rest but how to achieve this was another matter entirely. Before going to bed, King felt the urge to read something that would quiet his mind and "be a source of strength and inspiration."[5] He found it in *Margaret Ogilvie* by J.M. Barrie, author of the immortal *Peter Pan*. In the last chapter of *Margaret Ogilvie*, he found the following words: "Do you fear that He will not provide?" King interpreted the question as a message sent "direct to help me in this time of strain and to assure me of God's guidance."

Mackenzie King, of course, was altogether too perceptive to rely solely on the support of Divinity. To King there was a real possibility now that Ralston was determined to press his demand to send the conscripts overseas. It was an ultimatum that King was sure Ralston would back up with the threat of his resignation, thus splitting the Cabinet, and worst of all perhaps taking other ministers with him, a real possibility that must be avoided at all costs. A manoeuvre began to take shape in King's fertile mind. His thoughts turned to General Andrew George Latta McNaughton, the magnetic personality who had led the first Canadian troops to Britain in 1939. McNaughton had returned to Canada after being removed from his command in December 1943, because of failing health. At least, that was what the public had been told. In truth, McNaughton had lost the confidence of the Imperial General Staff in Britain and the support of his immediate boss, Defence Minister Ralston. When he had sailed off to war, McNaughton was cloaked in an aura of esteem and prestige. Now in October 1944, he found himself back in Canada beached and discarded by a nation that only months before had idolized him. McNaughton was an extraordinary character, and as the conscription crisis grew in intensity, fate and Mackenzie King's superb skill at political management placed McNaughton in the wings ready to play a starring role in the crisis.

Andy McNaughton was a portrait painter's dream. His leonine head looked as if it had been chiselled, somebody said, from a flawless piece of granite. The perfectly shaped temples, broad forehead, piercing eyes and resolute chin gave him a heroic presence. He was born in Moosomin, Saskatchewan, in 1887, to a prairie merchant. An electrical engineer, McNaughton served in World War I where he was wounded twice and mentioned in dispatches three times. He survived the war and became a brigadier at age thirty-one. He left the army briefly in the 1930s to serve as the head of the National Research Council in Ottawa. In fact, McNaughton was more of the scholar than the soldier. He looked on war as a science problem and the battlefield a laboratory. He forever searched to improve weaponry and equipment and fathered numerous innovative inventions to enhance the fighting man's chances of survival, ranging from a mobile laboratory to identify poison gas if it was ever used against troops, to the development of a flame thrower, to ways to waterproof airfield runways. But his tactical judgement, in the eyes of the British high command, was decidedly suspect. He had endorsed the Dieppe raid and by all accounts had made a mess of a large-scale exercise in Britain called Spartan. Finally, he split with Ralston on the question of whether to send Canadian troops into Italy. McNaughton firmly believed that when Canadians went into battle, they should go as a single force, not part of some other Allied command. When he was relieved of his command, his career rested in limbo.

Ironically, the day Ralston had departed for his European tour, King had met with McNaughton to discuss his future. McNaughton was on sick leave and King, despite the old general's questionable field skills, was entertaining the suggestion of promoting him to full general. He was also working over in his mind the idea of appointing McNaughton as the first Canadian-born governor-general. After Ralston's personal report on conditions at the battle front, King suddenly changed his mind on this lofty appointment for the general, and cruelly—there can be no other word—seized on the idea of using McNaughton as pawn in the rapidly deteriorating political chess game over conscription. In McNaughton, King found a willing ally. Andy McNaughton, despite his scientific genius, was ambitious and an incredibly vain man. Landing McNaughton was as easy as jigging for cod. Faced with Ralston's possible resignation, King plotted his next move:

> Should Ralston press his position to the point of resignation, my thought at the moment is to ask Gen. McNaughton to come into the government as Minister of Defence. The whole business really goes back to the struggle between Ralston and McNaughton: the separation of the Army for Italy at Ralston's insistence as against McNaughton and Churchill's wishes at the time. It is now clear that had the army been kept intact in England, there would be no need for reinforcements at this stage. If Ralston learns that McNaughton will be the one to take his place as the head of the army, if he does not fall in line with others, I doubt very much

if he will tender his resignation. I must at all costs avoid Canada being made a battlefield of civil strife at this stage of the war. I prayed very earnestly for guidance and strength in this crisis.[6]

When the War Committee met the following day, Thursday, October 19, Ralston reiterated the findings he had reported in private to the prime minister. When he finished, King quietly studied the faces of his ministers before speaking. He reminded them that the question was the most serious one that had come before Cabinet since Confederation, telling them he hoped they fully understood the import of Ralston's request for reinforcements: that Parliament would have to be recalled (it wasn't sitting at this time); that there was the prospect of bitter debate; and that if the question came to be decided by an election, the issue would be delayed sixty days as required by the Elections Act. It would be well into the new year before any results were known. "In the meantime," King continued, "it was certain that the most bitter kind of campaign would be waged from one end of Canada to the other. We would have province set against province in the central part of the Dominion. Other parts of Canada also divided."[7] But King saved his most ominous words for the conclusion of his reply to Ralston, asking the ministers how they thought the country would view the introduction of conscription at the end of five years of war. Then he told them "the issue was likely to create civil war." Ralston did not reply directly, but instead asked that General Stuart be called in to make his report.

There was no denying the uneviable position the chief of the Canadian headquarters overseas found himself in. It was obvious that there had been either a cover-up attempt to disguise the casualty figures, or just wholesale military staff bungling. King, of course, recognized the general's untenable position, and as Stuart delivered his gloomy assessment, King said he expected the general would now help the government out of the crisis. King was not above turning the screws a little tighter as the general proceeded with his report:

I asked Stuart if there was anything he wished to say. He mentioned having regretted he had to bring the report he did but that was his duty to state the situation as he saw it, etc. I mentioned that in considering it, he and his staff would remember that the whole question would have to come before Parliament which might debate it at great length. There might then have to be a general election and that it would be on into the new year before [a] decision could be reached. It would be best to consider if there was not some way that the situation could be met without all this turmoil and strife before the end of the year. I asked Stuart about his statement, his assurance 2 months ago as to there being plenty of reinforcements, and also about the additional brigade in Italy not making any additional drain on manpower. He gave some sort of an explanation about the latter that it simply meant changing over certain units; did not touch the question of extra men involved. As to the former, he said he had made a mistake. Later I said to him that having given us the wrong information and having made a mistake, I hoped he would, as I know he would, do all he could to help the govt. out of the present situation.[8]

Stuart's report left them all quiet and sombre, except for Ralston, who began debating some points. King deftly defused a confrontation with his defence minister at this time, saying the issue was too grave to try to settle immediately. Besides he wanted all the ministers present. They agreed to break until the following day, Friday. Before meeting the War Committee the next day, King huddled with St. Laurent who agreed with King that conscription would be calamitous, and besides there was no necessity from the point of view of winning the war. King further took St. Laurent into his confidence, telling him of his plans to bring in McNaughton to replace Ralston if he decided to bolt. St. Laurent approved of the strategy. When the War Committee sat, an irritable Ralston, for the first time, directly challenged King on the issue, reminding the prime minister that he had given his pledge to impose conscription if necessary, and the present and indisputable facts meant the time had come. King fired back that there would be no conscripting the Zombies or anyone else. Strangely, Ralston retreated. The questions were left dangling until the following Tuesday when the Cabinet as a whole would be available. But there was no doubt at all in King's mind that Ralston would change his position. "There is something inhumanly determined about his getting his own way regardless of what the effects may be on all others," King wrote in his diary.[9]

Mackenzie King spent the weekend brooding over the issues, except for a few hours of relief on Saturday. Into the midst of this drama, there appeared in Ottawa at a victory loan campaign — and it was completely ludicrous — the sparkling figure of Shirley Temple of the "Good Ship Lollipop" fame. King was instantly smitten by the attractive Temple. Following a rally on Parliament Hill, King escorted Temple to the Chateau Laurier where he was nearly crushed by Temple's adoring fans. King rescued the movie moppet, whisking her into an elevator to escape the crush of fans. They lunched together and King invited Temple and her parents to tea at Laurier House that evening.

By Tuesday King was back on the firing line to face another indescribable week of anxiety and tension as Ralston, unshakeable in his decision not to abandon the call for conscription, hammered home his points once more. By Wednesday, October 25, Ralston had succeeded in sowing doubt in the minds of some of the Cabinet members that there may well be no other choice than conscription. Ilsley, minister of finance, and Macdonald, minister for naval services, seemingly had come to Ralston's side — Howe, too, perhaps. That night, King pondered what tomorrow's tactics would be, certain that Ralston would announce his resignation the next day.

When King expressed his sentiments to Power, the minister for air and still a fierce anti-conscriptionist informed his leader that, if asked, he would not take the position (defence minister). "Little does he know," King wrote in his diary, "that he would be the last person I would ask today in this crisis."[10] Power's continued drinking disgusted King. The show-down on the issue had been played out the summer before in August 1943, at the Quebec Conference where King had gone to meet Churchill and Roosevelt. At the height of the conference, King's spies informed him that Power had arrived in the Quebec capital and was seen roaring drunk in a hotel corridor, crawling on his hands and knees without any trousers on. Moreover, he had confiscated the hotel's last three bottles of whisky. When King confronted Power a few days later, he demanded that Chubby take the pledge, which he did. But, alas, not for long. The last person King wanted as defence minister was Chubby Power. Even though he was possibly King's staunchest anti-conscriptionist, he was passé.

As the interminable debate continued, King, clutching at straws, assigned Pickersgill to provide the latest figures on just how many men were in army uniform in Canada. When Pickersgill handed King the list, the chief was astonished. Pickersgill reported there were 130,000 men in Canada who had volunteered to serve anywhere. At least that was Pickersgill's recollection many years after the event. In fact, the numbers were considerably greater. In Canada alone there were 120,000 general service men and another 90,000 more serving in England. Besides the volunteers, there were in the ranks of the Zombies a total of 68,489, although nearly 9,000 were on extended leave. On Thursday, October 26, King confronted Ralston with the figures saying surely out of this combined force, the army could convince 15,000 of the soldiers to volunteer, which was the number that General Stuart assessed as being necessary to make up the required replacements. "His reply," recorded King, "was the time was short. He was satisfied we could not get them. He had tried recruiting; others had tried, etc. I said we have not yet tried the recruiting by government. We have not yet attempted to see what we can do by extra inducements to the men."[11] Ralston remained obstinately convinced that time had run out to get anyone to volunteer. Besides, he had said earlier that most of the general service men, although they had volunteered, were not properly trained, and that was what was needed at the battle front. There were too many truck drivers, clerks and cooks. What was desperately needed were trained infantrymen, and that in the ranks of the Zombies there were at least 30,000 trained field soldiers, not rear echelon types. King found the situation impossible to believe. "He wasn't the only one," said Pickersgill many years later. "I went over those figures over and over again because I had been keeping track of them all the time. I found it utterly incredible and I find it incredible to this day."[12] In desperation King even cabled Charles De Gaulle to see if he was willing to supply Free French troops to make up the needed reinforcements in the French-Canadian fighting regiments.

Someone else suggested the government institute a lottery. When a volunteer's name came up, he would be assigned as one of 15,000 replacements.

Another insider, General Maurice Pope, military secretary to the War Committee of the Cabinet, took it upon himself to try to convince Ralston to stay on. "I asked him," said Pope, "if he didn't have a greater duty towards Canada. He said his position was very uncomfortable. . . . I went even further and told him that when a man reached high office his future often lay in the hands of the whims of fortune, and that through no fault of his own, his career might come to an end. There was a glimpse in his eye at one moment as if he could see some way out of the dilemma, but he didn't give utterance to it and then I took my leave of him. It was a very critical moment, I thought, in the history of our country."[13]

By Tuesday, October 31, King's nerves may have been stretched to their limit, but his political instincts were as deadly as ever. The time had come to dispose of Ralston. King summoned Andy McNaughton to Laurier House. Shortly after noon, King ushered McNaughton into his library. Before the comforting flame of the open fireplace, King struck a deal with McNaughton; as the logs crackled and hissed, he sealed Ralston's fate forever. To McNaughton, King said this:

> I outlined to him in strict confidence the present situation. I began by saying to him I felt the need of his counsel and advice. What I was telling him was in absolute confidence and that I needed guidance with respect to some of the matters that had to be considered. I said I knew no one who could give it to me as well as himself.
>
> I told him what I thought of Ralston's recommendation and something of Stuart's report. He said to me Stuart was quite wrong in making a recommendation as to policy. He agreed that reinforcements were not necessary for the winning of the war, and I spoke of our having been told in August that all was well, that we were under that impression throughout the Quebec Conference. It was only since Ralston returned that we discovered he

had had a message from Crerar* expressing concern about the need for reinforcements. He said that that was quite wrong. I then mentioned to him that I thought Ralston would resign and that I did not see any other person in sight but himself to take the position of Minister of Defence. That I believed if he were Minister he would be able to get things worked out in such a way that we would not need to resort to conscription for overseas service. He was strongly of the belief that the conscription issue in Canada would work irreparable harm.

He finally said to me that if Ralston did resign, he would be at my disposition and prepared to take on the task. He said he would get rid of Stuart and Murchie.** That Murchie had never taken part in any operations. He did not trust their judgment. He mentioned one or two other new men who had come over who he thought might be helpful. I told him I would be glad to be out altogether for a while. He said to me, but you will have to stay at all costs. He said that I should not get out at this time. I said I would not so long as other situations would be saved. I then asked him about other members of the Cabinet; how he got along with Power and Angus Macdonald. He said very well with both; never had any differences with them and would get on well. I asked about Howe. He said he had been lunching with Howe yesterday, that they were very friendly. I told him that Howe had suggested to me at one stage to bring him in. That Mackenzie*** had said the same; Gardiner† the same. St. Laurent agreed it would be wise.

McNaughton agreed nothing would be said about the matter until I saw him again but left with the understanding that I could definitely count on him. He said at the elevator that if he came in, it would be a major sensation, a matter of world significance.[14]

In that regard, the old soldier was right on target. For Mackenzie King, his timing was once again impeccable. As McNaughton left Laurier House, he confessed to King that he had been talking with

---

*General Harry Crerar, the Canadian Army Commander, now in hospital in England because of recurring bouts of dysentery.
**General J.C. Murchie, Chief of General Staff, Ottawa.
***Ian Mackenzie, minister of pensions and national health.
†James C. Gardiner, minister of agriculture.

some of Canada's celebrated Tories, who wished him to join forces
with them to unseat the Liberals. Now, McNaughton said, he would
have to inform them he was being given a greater opportunity to serve
his country in its time of need. King assured him he was making the
right decision.

CHAPTER THIRTEEN

Betrayal

ITH ANDY McNAUGHTON SEQUESTERED in the flies of the Cabinet's crowded stage, Mackenzie King stepped from the wings for one last performance before his bickering and anxious players. Ralston, always the villain in King's mind, repeated his familiar chant to send the Zombies overseas. Little did he know that earlier on that last day in October, King the impresario, like some sleazy film mogul, had just signed up a new star to replace him. But the time had not quite arrived. Instead, King confronted Ralston once more. Would he take the responsibility of forming a government? No, Ralston replied. Then what of the others? King asked. Ilsley? Macdonald? Any others? All the replies came in the negative. Someone suggested leaving the matter over until tomorrow. King spoke of the possibility of calling Parliament together in the near future. He would like the night to himself to think about it. They all agreed to meet the following afternoon. King returned to Laurier House, dined alone, and later in the evening met George Zaroubin, the Soviet ambassador. Zaroubin had come to invite King to dinner the following evening, but the prime minister replied that

pressing business prevented him from accepting. King retired when
Zaroubin departed, but slept little. By morning he had made his decision. McNaughton was summoned to Laurier House once again, and
once more King elicited from the general his support that conscription
was not necessary; together they would appeal to the Zombies and
others to volunteer as replacements. Next stop on this first day of
November was Government House where King informed the Earl of
Athlone it was most likely that he would get Ralston's resignation that
afternoon and to approve a recommendation to appoint McNaughton
as the new minister of national defence. By mid-afternoon King was
back before Cabinet, but it was not until 6:00 P.M. that he quietly lobbed
his bombshell into the proceedings:

> I then said I thought we ought to, if possible, reach a conclusion
> without further delay; that I had been told each day that an hour's
> delay would prejudice the securing of men; I did not see [that]
> would get any further by not getting an understanding at once.
> After what was said last night I realized that some way would
> have to be found, if it could be found, to save the government
> and to save a terrible division at this time, and at the same time
> make sure of getting reinforcement if that was possible at all.
> That I had been asking myself was there anyone who could do
> this; who believed that our policy, which had worked successfully
> for five years, would now work for the remaining weeks or months
> of the war. If there was, I thought it was owing to the country
> that such a person's services would be secured. I said I believed
> I had the man who could undertake that task and carry it out. I
> then mentioned General McNaughton's name and said that there
> was no man in whom the troops overseas would feel their interests
> were being more taken care of than McNaughton. That there was
> no man toward whom the mothers and fathers throughout this
> country would have the same feeling more strongly; that there
> was no man in whom the citizens of Canada as a whole would
> have greater confidence for a task of that kind. McNaughton had
> taken no part in politics; was not a Liberal, a Conservative, or
> C.C.F., though he was very liberal-minded and very liberal in
> his policies. There was a difference between a campaign being
> started by a man who had little faith in what could be accomplished
> and by one who believed if he put his heart into it he could secure

results. Ralston had said that while he was prepared to speak he did not think it would be of much effect. That I knew McNaughton felt otherwise; that he believed that tackled in the right way he himself could find the men necessary for reinforcements by the voluntary method. . . .

I then said that the people of Canada would say that McNaughton was the right man for the task, and since Ralston had clearly said that he himself did not believe we could get the men without conscription, while McNaughton believed we could, and that he, Ralston, would have to tender his resignation, as he had said at different times he would do if we pressed eliminating the conscription part; that I thought if Ralston felt in that way, he should make it possible for us to bring him in to the Cabinet at once—the man who was prepared to see this situation through. I said that in regard to a resignation from Ralston, that he had tendered his resignation to me some two years ago and had never withdrawn it; that that had been a very trying thing for me to go on day in and day out for this period with this resignation not withdrawn, but simply held. I then drew attention to the fact that no one could say that McNaughton was not the best person who could be secured. I drew from my pockets the exchange of letters, as printed, in September last, in which there is a statement that they have not seen eye to eye on some matters, but each shared the belief in the others sincerity of conviction. I read the passage in which Ralston had made plain what McNaughton had done in training, etc.; his great skill, and certainty of his desire to serve Canada. I said there could be no misunderstanding as to McNaughton's qualifications. . . .

I concluded by saying that I thought we ought not to allow this situation to drag on at all. The strongest of reasons had been given repeatedly why it should not, and that I thought we should decide at once what was to be done. There was intense silence.

Then Ralston spoke very quietly. He said that he would of course give me his resignation at once. He wished to thank me for the opportunity given him to serve. I had referred to having asked Ralston long ago to come into the Cabinet; that he had made great sacrifices. I had asked him before the war. He had said he could not, but if the war came, he would, and he did immediately. That I did not think any man had served the country more faithfully in every way or given the best of everything he had. Ralston went on to say that he had done the best he possibly could. He knew he was limited in some things, but had done his best. He spoke of the companionship we had enjoyed and what it meant to share in the work with his colleagues; that he sincerely hoped the new Minister — I forgot how he referred to him — I think he said the new move — might be successful. He was not sure that it would be but he certainly hoped it would. He ended by saying that he would retire to private life. I replied that no words could express what we felt of his integrity, service, and the like; that it would be mere heroics to use any words regarding what we all knew so well. This was not a personal matter; it was what the situation at the moment seemed to demand. I thanked him for all he had done, and again expressed how hard it was for me to say what I felt I had to say in the interests of Canada's war effort.

Ralston then gathered up his papers and turned to me and shook hands. I have forgotten what he said. I think it was: he thanked me for the opportunity he had had. All the Cabinet rose, formed a complete circle around the table, and shook hands with him. As he was going out the door I called to him that I wanted to have just a further word. I had spoken of the desirability of having the new appointment made at the same time as Ralston's resignation was accepted. I hoped that might be done this evening and have the matter cleared up today. At the door, I asked him whether it would be possible to let me have his resignation tonight. He had said he would write out his resignation. He looked very anxious and strained and said could he have until the morning. I said by all means but to please say nothing about it to any one; to keep the matter wholly secret and confidential, until the other appointment was made. This he said he would do.[1]

It's tempting to speculate whether any political figure before or since had been hoisted so high with his own petard as was Ralston. King's masterful use of Ralston's own letters of endorsement was brilliant courtroom theatrics. It wasn't enough to simply impale Ralston, King strangled him with his own words. Of course, it was also a dangerous execution for there was no guarantee that Ralston would remain idle in disgrace. He could still bolt the party and cross the floor. Yet that was a risk King was to take. Anyway, there was no time to lose.

McNaughton immediately took to the streets to drum up volunteers. In his first public speech since his appointment as defence minister, McNaughton told a testy crowd in the Ottawa Valley town of Arnprior that he favoured the system of voluntary enlistment now in force and that he was confident "our men and women will come forward to serve — that they will take up this gallant honourable obligation and rally to support our gallant comrades overseas."[2] The audience was shocked. They couldn't believe the respected General McNaughton, known as the father of the Canadian Army, was abandoning the fighting men on the battlefield. A number of angry veterans confronted the general point-blank, demanding to know his intentions regarding getting the Zombies into action. His replies were evasive. The next night, November 6, McNaughton met an even more hostile audience. He had gone to the National Museum auditorium in Ottawa to speak before 800 veterans and servicemen. Again he steadfastly defended King's policy of no conscription for overseas service. But his avowals were met by frequent and derisive interjections. "Give the Zombies guts! . . . Send the Zombies over . . . What about the British and U.S. draft?" hecklers shouted at the shaken general.[3] Had King misunderstood the depth of resentment against the Zombies? On November 8, King took to the airwaves with his own personal plea in a dramatic appeal that came to be known as his "Race of Warriors" speech.

> The glory of Canada's fight for freedom is the imperishable fact that every Canadian in uniform at sea, in the air and on every fighting front is there by his own choice. In this world conflict Canada has produced a race of noble warriors. The light in their eyes is the light of liberty, and the fire in their hearts is the fire of spirits dedicated to the service of their fellow-men.
>
> This is not the hour to destroy that magnificent record. It is the hour to kindle the fire of free service in the hearts of all our young men in the army and outside its ranks.
>
> To you, young men, who are serving in Canada's "home defence" forces, I should like to make a special appeal.
>
> Because of the training you have already received, you are in an exceptional position to give service which is particularly needed at this time. I have told you of the need. Let me emphasize the opportunity — the greatest you will ever have — to further serve your country and to bring honour to yourselves and your families. You will never regret the decision to do all you possibly can to support Canada's fighting army.

In doing that, you will be helping to destroy the enemy of mankind and to provide security and opportunity for yourselves, your children and your fellow-men. You will be doing more than that. You will be helping to remove a source of misunderstanding, bitterness and division in our own country and to preserve its strength through years to come. You will be helping to lay the foundations of a better world.

I appeal no less earnestly to the friends and families of our young men to help and encourage them in a decision which will mean everything to them through the rest of their lives.[4]

Instead of rallying Canadians, King's appeal seemed only to deepen their anxiety. What the people heard was not a plan for solving the shortage of trained reinforcements, but a pathetically confused confession by the government of its own worst fears and suspicions. Why not send the Zombies? newspaper editorials asked. By King's own admission there were plenty of fully trained Zombies, equipped and ready for combat. No one bought the argument, either, that there was some abstract honour at stake by having only volunteers fight. The *Globe* charged that King reached his emotional peak in his plea for keeping the Canadian Army completely voluntary, but ignored what the whole world knew—that the ranks of British and American armies were largely made up of draftees.

In his radio address, King had also announced that Parliament would meet November 22, by which time he had hoped his and McNaughton's pleas would result in the necessary volunteer replacements of properly trained men. At first, King was convinced the appeal was going to be effective. But on November 12, Ralston broke his silence with a statement to the press about why he had resigned. In private, King accused Ralston of disclosing military secrets. Worse, the Cabinet remained split and by the middle of the month, King was gripped with fear that at least two ministers might follow Ralston, naming in his diary Macdonald and Ilsley. On November 14, there was more bad news. McNaughton reported that his appeal "was not as satisfactory as I should have liked."[5] That was the same day the army brass concluded there was little hope of obtaining volunteers. Five days later, on November 19, reports from four district army commanders from across the country indicated the appeal was doomed to fail. Two days later, as the atmosphere went from bad to worse, King himself plunged into a black depression, writing he "felt very depressed at the thought of the appalling situation into which I was being drawn and fearful lest my physical strength and nervous strength might not stand the strain."[6] Later that day he told a startled Cabinet that he himself was going to resign. When the stunned ministers recovered, they pleaded with King to stay—reading between the lines, a plea made not so much as a vote of confidence in King but in sheer desperation, for their own minds were numbed by intense fatigue.

It didn't seem possible, but more debilitating news was about to be delivered to the beleaguered Mackenzie King. According to Bruce Hutchison, King's telephone rang at twelve noon on November 22. On the line was Andy McNaughton, who in a hoarse rasp informed King: "I have terrible news for you, Chief! What I must tell you will come as a body blow."[7] There was a distinct possibility of a revolt by a cabal of army officers. King was incredulous. This was not some banana republic where disgruntled generals were likely to stage a revolution. This was Canada! The idea of fat, bemedalled generals seizing radio stations and taking over Parliament Hill was ludicrous.

What in fact happened was a threat of resignation by principal staff officers that made up what was called the Army Council. In the best bureaucratic fashion, the threat was veiled. Unless conscription was immediately imposed, they could not accept responsibility for directing Army affairs. A few days earlier, a number of brigadiers and lieutenant-colonels in Pacific Command had openly criticized King's stand to the press. This, combined with McNaughton's latest news about the possibility of mass resignation of the Army Council, created spectacular reaction on Parliament Hill. General Pope remembered "that very day I heard in the East Block the expression 'a palace revolution.' "[8]

Whether King truly believed an Army revolt was at hand remains a question no one can answer. Years later, Walter Turnbull said there was no such possibility. "But," he added, " a lot of people thought there was. Whether he [King] believed it or not, or whether he was really using that to frighten the children, and say gather around father, the wolves are at the door, I don't know. He could believe things, but he also said a lot of things under the emotional stress that he didn't really believe in. He wouldn't have believed them the next day.''[9]

At the height of this incredible drama, King had been handed one last straw to clutch. He seized it. Hadn't he always said conscription if necessary, but not necessarily conscription? Now, he had been given an exit from the burning stage, whose fire he himself had ignited because of his obsession that conscription would create civil war. His thinking, although convoluted, was perfectly clear. To prevent dismemberment of the country, he would accede to the generals' demands and impose conscription. He would deal with the generals later. First, he must convince Louis St. Laurent. After hearing King's reasoning, the Quebec minister expressed astonishment of an army take-over. But King was at his persuasive best. He convinced the one man who stood between survival and utter defeat. King knew if he secured St. Laurent's approval as a French-speaking Canadian, Quebecers would conclude that conscription was now perhaps necessary. St. Laurent agreed there was no other course. At three o'clock that afternoon the House met, the correspondence dealing with Ralston's resignation was read, and while the Tories wanted immediate debate, the C.C.F. and Social Credit party demanded time to study the documents. It was agreed by all to adjourn the House early. That evening, the Cabinet met and learned to their immense relief from Andy McNaughton that because sufficient numbers of volunteers had failed to answer the government's appeal, he now recommended that 16,000 Zombies be sent overseas at once. Only Chubby Power objected, informing his colleagues that he was obliged to resign.

The following day, November 23, 1944, a draft of the order-in-council was ready for King's approval. Shortly after three o'clock the House assembled and Mackenzie King rose to speak. In his flat, monotonous voice he informed the members: ''I desire to read to the House an order-in-council which sets forth the policy of the government with respect to the extension of service of N.R.M.A. personnel, which order is P.C. 8891, and has been approved by His Excellency the Governor-General today.''[10]

The Zombies — 16,000 of them — were being ordered into battle.

It was doubtful the news was of any comfort to thousands of Canadian families. From October 1 to November 8, as Mackenzie King plotted his survival, death had stalked the freezing polders of the Scheldt Estuary. During that period 6,467 Canadians had been reported killed, wounded or missing.

Epilogue

Man of Granite

O N JANUARY 3, 1945, the first draft of Zombies sailed from Halifax for the battlefields of Europe. By war's end nearly 13,000 were serving overseas but, unlike the volunteers, the Zombie casualties were light. There were a number of reasons for this. The Allied planners had decided to transfer the Canadians in Italy to northwest Europe, a move which kept them out of the battle line for many weeks. When the Germans launched their last big offensive in the Ardennes in mid-December, it delayed the First Canadian Army's planned operation, called "Veritable," for nearly five weeks between the Maas and the Rhine. As a result, there were fewer casualties. Sixty-nine of them never made it home. Yet, for all the drama, it was curious how little trouble there was when conscription was finally enforced. There were a few incidents in some army camps when Zombies challenged the order; others went over the hill and although most eventually returned to duty, a few hundred went into exile in their own country. Only recently one aging and toothless Zombie emerged from the woods of Nova Scotia to give himself up, much like the occasional Japanese soldier who crept back to civilization from the jungles of Pacific isles during the 1960s and '70s.

The strife that Mackenzie King so feared would break out in Quebec once conscription was imposed never did materialize and never got beyond mild protest. When the time came to vote on the issue, nineteen French-speaking members supported King. And although Canadian flyers, sailors and soldiers still faced a determined enemy, it was clear by the spring of 1945 that the conflict was nearing its bitter finale. At 1:41 A.M. on May 7, at Reims, France, all German forces surrendered unconditionally. At 7:00 A.M. in Ottawa, King was awakened by a servant who told him of the surrender. "Thank God," King said, then turned on his side and "uttered a prayer of thanksgiving and rededication to the service of my fellow-men."[1]

May 8 was proclaimed a public holiday, and under King's instructions the Canadian Red Ensign, the flag Canadians had carried to battle, was to be raised on Parliament Hill as a salute to the Canadian fighting men—a gesture King was sure would please them. What effect it had is hard to say. For a majority of the servicemen, King remained the object of their disgust because of his procrastination on the issue of conscription throughout the long conflict. This they demonstrated when Canada went to the polls on June 11, 1945, for its first national election since 1940. When the ballots were counted in his own riding of Prince Albert, King squeaked to victory with a narrow lead. Still to come were the ballots cast by the servicemen overseas.

By June 19, after all the ballots were totalled, King to his dismay discovered that he had lost and that the servicemen's vote probably made the difference between victory and defeat. He had suspected this might happen, for only three days before, he had written in his diary: "I kept going over in my thoughts what I should say in a letter to the constituents. I also felt in my heart a sense of sadness that the relationship which had existed over 19 years should now be severed by so few votes and particularly by votes from overseas service."[2] It was a bitter pill to swallow, but King remained confident he could regain a seat in a by-election. And that is what happened on August 6 when he became the member for Glengarry when the sitting member conveniently removed himself to make room for the prime minister.

Even though his Liberal government had been re-elected, a ghost of the conscription crisis continued to haunt Andy McNaughton. He was running out of ridings to contest. After being named defence minister, McNaughton had lost a by-election the previous February in North Grey. Then, in the June general election McNaughton went down to another defeat in the riding of Qu'Appelle.

There were so many victims in the wake of the conscription crisis, it is difficult to know where to start. McNaughton must share the centre stage of any examination. The soldiers had believed they had in McNaughton a champion. After all, he had come to be known as the father of the Canadian army. Yet, within hours of his appointment as defence minister, the old soldier announced his intention of supporting King's non-conscription policy. The one person who was capable of supporting the servicemen betrayed them at first opportunity. By the time he reversed himself, his own credibility was damaged beyond repair. He was, of course, the author of his own misfortune. Still smarting over his removal from commanding in the field, his willingness to join King's plot against Ralston certainly had an element of vengeance. Here was an opportunity to strike back at the man he believed was at least partly responsible for his public disgrace, James Layton Ralston. But his soldier's art was no match against the greatest politician in Canadian history. While McNaughton would enjoy a postwar career as a diplomat, he was also remembered as the general who became a pawn in King's conscription campaign. By August 1945, King realized McNaughton's inability to get elected seriously impaired his effectiveness. McNaughton came to the same conclusion, and on August 6, the day the atomic bomb was dropped on Hiroshima, McNaughton offered King his resignation. Rejected twice by the voters, there was no possibility now of becoming Canada's first Canadian-born governor-general. John Swettenham, McNaughton's biographer, said the general had become in his own mind the most hated man in Canada (although King claimed this distinction for himself). He departed in somewhat better circumstances than Ralston, being appointed to represent Canada as the chairman on a joint U.S.-Canadian defence board.

Layton Ralston departed with a complete break from public life after the crisis, returning to practise law in Montreal. Within a few years he was dead, some said of a broken heart and because of immense fatigue from his battles with Mackenzie King. He was remembered as the man who never betrayed the soldiers he had sent into battle. For this, he died a respected man. King attended his funeral, but Ralston's widow refused to receive him. The scars of her husband's political assassination were never to heal. Much has been written about the high risk King took in dispatching Ralston who, if he had chosen, could have destroyed King, his Liberal government, and could himself quite easily have become prime minister in union with the Conservative party. Bruce Hutchison said many years later that Ralston's "patriotism rose above any question of politics, [a man] who sacrificed himself and destroyed his career for what he regarded as public duty."[3] There is no doubt that King had recognized this quality in the man; it further confirms King's remarkable ability to judge character, not always in ideal or leisure surroundings but in the heat of battle. And that was the mark of an outstanding commander.

Chubby Power also made a graceful exit. His resignation in opposing conscription honoured the memory of the dead Ernest Lapointe, a man who would certainly have opposed King to the end. Power also kept the promise he had made to Quebecers. His relationship with King was never the same after he left Cabinet. Power ran as a candidate for the leadership of the Liberal party in 1948, but was defeated by St. Laurent, who had been personally anointed by King to succeed him. Besides, King despaired at Power's continued boozing and he could not quite forget that Power had deserted him in his darkest hour. In 1955, St. Laurent appointed Chubby to the Senate. He lived out his days much loved in both French and English Canada for his incredible record as minister for air during the war; this was a fitting tribute to his decency as a human being and his commitment as a politician. His breed was rare.

The political battles of the war had taken their toll on Mackenzie King. While he was never completely dispossessed of his numerous

skills, he was beginning to show his age when he finally resigned
November 15, 1948. He has become the subject of intense examination
ever since, especially for his role during the conscription crisis. Why
he changed his mind at the eleventh hour has never been satisfactorily
explained. As late as 1978, General Hugh Young, a member of the
Army Council during those dramatic days in November 1944, categorically denied there was the slightest chance of a rebellion by the
senior military officers. That view is shared by almost everyone who
has studied the records. Moreover, what had changed so significantly
from the beginning of the war in King's mind that conscription would
not ignite civil strife in 1944? For years he had set down these fears
in his diary again and again—the spectre of rioting in the streets as
had occurred in 1917. Quite clearly his leadership was at stake, his
government in peril, and the imposition of conscription became in his
mind the only alternative in order to save himself and the government.
There was no other logic to the decision. For nearly five years, he
remained adamant that if conscription was enforced, national unity
would be destroyed. Then, overnight, he came to a new and inspired
belief that by enforcing conscription, he was assuring national unity.

Whatever the case, when King finally imposed conscription, his
circle of betrayal was complete: to Quebec for breaking his vows, and
to English Canada for delaying the decision that most certainly had
caused part of the high casualties on the battle front. Logistically, the
departure of the Zombies from Canada to Europe in the last months
of the war was of little value. While fighting continued during that
winter, its intensity never equalled the level it had reached in the fall
of 1944. Besides, there had been time for the infantry to recuperate
in northwest Europe where it was now dug in along a 200-mile front
holding the ground it had so preciously won, and to prepare the final
offensive in the spring. The Zombies were too late. They had been
needed in the summer of 1944 when vicious fighting raged in Italy
and in the Normandy bridgehead. And for the Zombies to have found
themselves in those places at that time would have required conscription
for overseas service almost from the beginning of the war.

Exactly how much King contributed to the high casualty rate because
of his procrastination is of course impossible to know. Who could walk

through the well-groomed military cemeteries in Italy and France or Holland today and say that the occupant of this grave, or that grave, was the direct victim of King's complicated, and sometimes devious, delaying tactics throughout the war? Any unit can remain effective as long as its casualties are replaced with properly trained reinforcements, even men without combat experience, so long as they are fully trained and are given the opportunity of being eased and guided into battle by experienced NCOs and company commanders. But when units were reduced forty per cent below strength, as many of them were, and faced with absorbing rear echelon soldiers only partially trained, calamity resulted. Of all the fighting services, the army accounted for the most casualties. By war's end, total casualties numbered 74,374, nearly 23,000 of them fatal. How much those casualties could have been lessened, given early conscription, is impossible to calculate. For those who fought, however, there is no question that the number of wounded or killed could have been considerably less. This they firmly believed; they also believed that they had been betrayed by their prime minister. The bitterness of many thousands of veterans has not diminished over nearly fifty years.

Mackenzie King visited the Normandy battlefield in August 1946. On August 10, his party left Paris for a two-day tour of the battle sites and Canadian cemeteries. Driving through a drizzling rain, the prime minister was greeted like a conquering hero wherever he stopped. The mayors of the villages of Normandy spoke of the profound sacrifice on the part of the Canadian fighting man; youngsters in their Sunday best presented King with numerous bouquets of flowers. At Bretteville-sur-Laize, the prime minister was driven to one of the many Canadian cemeteries dotting the Norman landscape. "It lies peacefully under the open sky in the centre of a wide stretch of open country," wrote King in his diary. "In part of it the grass has grown between the graves; in other parts grass has still to be sown. Each little grave had its separate mound, all uniform in shape. It touched me deeply to see between the graves that were named, here and there, one simply classified as unknown soldier. We took the flowers that had been given to us at other centres and placed them before the Cross of Sacrifice which is in the middle of the cemetery. The sun was shining brightly. Looking at the crosses, in one way they were in shadow; the other very white against the sun. I found it quite impossible to give any expression to my feelings. Indeed, as I said, I felt silence was the only language in such a place."[4]

After his retirement in 1948, Mackenzie King returned to his beloved Kingsmere in the Gatineau Hills, where he lived out his remaining years quietly and, in every regard, alone. On a summer night in 1950, Mackenzie King died in his sleep in his brass bed in the upstairs bedroom of his farmhouse. The date was July 22, and when he died at eighteen minutes to ten, for once the hands of the clock were not in perfect alignment.

Historians continue to debate the mystery that was Mackenzie King, his most fervent supporters criticizing petulant critics for focusing on his eccentricities and his unattractive, pudgy figure, rather than on his legislative achievements which, while not a part of this narrative, were indeed considerable. Of course, all of this criticism is valid. But equally impressive was the man's determined leadership as Canada's wartime prime minister. To the last, however, he remained totally contradictory. While he could display gestures of kindness, sympathy and social grace, King was demonstrably able to be mean, cruel, cold-blooded and ruthless, an incredible mix of emotions which, when examined in the light of his fervently held religious beliefs, continues to puzzle all who study his life. Certainly there were no others in his government with the skill and the determination required to lead a country through its darkest hours. In the end, Mackenzie King won his war, but only because the depth of resolve of many thousands of brave Canadian men and women was as heroic as the man they followed into battle.

SELECT CHRONOLOGY

1874

December 17   King born at Berlin (now Kitchener) Ontario

1937

June 29   King meets Adolf Hitler in Berlin, Germany

1939

September 1   Germany invades Poland; World War II begins
September 10   Canada declares war on Germany
October 25   Premier Duplessis defeated in Quebec provincial election
                   after challenging King's wartime leadership
December 17   King signs agreement with Britain establishing the British
                   Commonwealth Air Training Plan in Canada

1940

March 26   King's wartime government re-elected after Premier Hep-
                   burn of Ontario questions King's wartime conduct of
                   affairs
June 18   King introduces the National Resources Mobilization Act
                   requiring Canadians to register for national service within
                   Canada
July 5   James Layton Ralston becomes minister of defence

1941

November 26   Ernest Lapointe, King's justice minister, dies
December 7   Japanese attack Pearl Harbor
December 10   Louis S. St. Laurent succeeds Lapointe as justice minister
December 25   Hong Kong surrenders after heavy fighting; survivors of
                   two Canadian army battalions imprisoned in Japanese
                   POW camps

1942

February 9   Newly appointed Conservative leader Arthur Meighen,
                   calling for conscription, is defeated in Toronto's South
                   York by-election
March 4   Order-in-council authorizing relocation of Japanese Cana-
                   dians on west coast goes into effect
April 27   National plebiscite gives King a free hand on conscription
May 9   P.J.A. Cardin, minister of public works, resigns over
                   Bill 80

161

July 7	Bill 80 passes second reading in Parliament giving government power to conscript, amending the NRMA
August 19	Canadian troops go into battle with raid on the French seaport town of Dieppe; thousands killed, wounded, missing or captured

1943

July 10	Canadian troops part of Allied force that invades Sicily, the beginning of the Italian campaign
December 27	Gen. A. G. L. McNaughton hands over command of the First Canadian Army to his successor; his abilities to command in the field are questioned

1944

June 6	Canadian troops part of Allied force that invades Normandy
September 19	Major Conn Smythe returns wounded from France, charging untrained troops are being sent into battle because of a lack of properly trained replacements
September 24	Defence Minister Ralston leaves for personal inspection of battle situation in Italy, France, Belgium and Holland
October 18	Defence Minister Ralston returns to Canada convinced that only conscription can supply the required and properly trained men needed to replace mounting casualties
November 1	King fires Ralston as defence minister, replacing him with Gen. McNaughton
November 8	King makes national appeal on radio to soldiers conscripted for Home service to volunteer for overseas
November 22	Gen. McNaughton reports the Army High Command might resign if conscription is not imposed to send conscripts, called "Zombies," into battle
November 23	King reverses his policy of no conscription for overseas service, tabling in the Commons an order-in-council to draft 16,000 Zombies for service at the front
November 27	Minister for Air Charles Gavan "Chubby" Power resigns from King's Cabinet in protest against overseas conscription
December 7	King's government survives confidence motion in Parliament on conscription policy

1945

January 3	First of the Zombie conscripts leave Halifax for overseas

February 5	Gen. McNaughton loses by-election in his attempt for the North Grey seat in the House
April 13	King dissolves Parliament
May 8	Germany surrenders
June 11	King's Liberal government returned to power in general election, but King loses his seat in the riding of Prince Albert; McNaughton loses his second attempt to gain seat in the Commons in the riding of Qu'Appelle
August 6	King re-elected in by-election in the riding of Glengarry; atomic bomb is dropped on Hiroshima; and McNaughton offers King his resignation
August 14	Japan surrenders, ending World War II

1948

November 15	King resigns as prime minister

1950

July 22	King dies in bed at Kingsmere at age seventy-six

SOURCE NOTES

The following abbreviations have been used in the source notes, under three categories: Books, Articles and Periodicals, and Other Sources. Remaining sources, such as newspaper articles, are identified in the notes themselves.

BOOKS

AC	Manchester, *American Caesar*
AH	Toland, *Adolf Hitler*
AM	Graham, *Arthur Meighen*
AMAG	Stacey, *Arms, Men and Governments*
AM (TC)	English, *Arthur Meighen (The Canadians)*
APP	Power, *A Party Politician*
AVDL	Stacey, *A Very Double Life*
AWIF	Malone, *A World in Flames*
BD	Shirer, *Berlin Diary*
CD	Roberts, *C.D. The Life and Times of Clarence Decatur Howe*
CDH	Bothwell, Kilbourne, *C.D. Howe*
CS	Smythe, *Conn Smythe*
CS: IYCBEITA	Smythe (Young), *Conn Smythe: If You Can't Beat 'Em in the Alley*
DA	Dunkelman, *Dual Allegiance*
Duplessis	Black, *Duplessis*
FFHRADIC	Berger, *Fragile Freedoms: Human Rights and Dispension in Canada*
IDOC	Eayrs, *In Defence of Canada*
ITTR	Speer, *Inside the Third Reich*
JGATNFB	Evans, *John Grierson and the National Film Board*
KOTHS	Esberey, *Knight of the Holy Spirit*
MH	McKenty, *Mitch Hepburn*
MKOC	Hardy, *Mackenzie King of Canada*
MK: WTD	English, Stubbs (Granatstein), *Mackenzie King: Widening the Debate*
MOG	Foster, *Meeting of Generals*
NITM	Abella, Troper, *None Is Too Many*
NRW	Vincent, *No Reason Why*
ODDATBFN	Hastings, *Overlord, D-Day and the Battle for Normandy*
ODTAA	Garner, *One Damned Thing After Another*
OTTR	Lamb, *On the Triangle Run*
RCNIR	Boutilier, *RCN in Retrospect*
SYOW	Stacey, *Six Years of War* (Vol. 1)
TBCWD	Middlebrook, Everitt, *The Bomber Command War Diaries*

164

TBP	Scott, Smith, *The Blasted Pine*
TCA	Stacey, *The Canadian Army*
TCN	Lamb, *The Corvette Navy*
TCOANAF	Douglas, *The Creation of a National Air Force*
TETNW	Adachi, *The Enemy That Never Was*
TGATD	Manchester, *The Glory and the Dream*
TIC	Hutchison, *The Incredible Canadian*
TMKR	Pickersgill, *The Mackenzie King Record* (Vol. 1)
TOW	Whitaker, D., and S., *Tug of War*
TPATPM	Martin, *The Presidents and the Prime Ministers*
TRAFOTTR	Shirer, *The Rise and Fall of the Third Reich*
TSATGD	Robertson, *The Shame and the Glory — Dieppe*
TWS	Bryan, Murphy, *The Windsor Story*
WLMK	Neatby, *William Lyon Mackenzie King* (Vol. II)

ARTICLES AND PERIODICALS

CDQ "Air Marshal Harold ('Gus') Edwards and the Canadian-ization of the RCAF Overseas, 1941-43" by Vincent G. Rigby. *Canadian Defence Quarterly*, Winter 1987.

"Canada's Navy 1910 to 1985" by Commander A.B. German, RCN (ret.) *Canadian Defence Quarterly*, December 1985.

"Morale in the Canadian Army in Canada during the Second World War" by Professor R.H. Roy, *Canadian Defence Quarterly*, Autumn 1986.

CHR "The Divine Mission: Mackenzie King and Hitler" by C.P. Stacey, *Canadian Historical Review*, LXI, 4, 1980.

FO "Fixed Obsession" by Ronald Blumer; research paper in six parts for the National Film Board of Canada, April 1986, for the six-hour television series, *King Chronicle*, broadcast March 1988, CBC-TV, and produced by Donald Brittain and Adam Symansky.

OTHER SOURCES

CBC-DBY Oral history interviews conducted by David Scrivens, Robert McKenzie, Geoff Scott, Brian Nolan, Cameron Graham, Jean Bruce and Larry Zolf, for the CBC historical-political television series *The Days Before Yesterday*, seven one-hour documentaries, broadcast the autumn of 1973 on CBC-TV. The date of each interview used in *King's War* is noted as it appears in the source notes.

KD The Mackenzie King Diaries 1923-1949 (Microfiche edition), University of Toronto Press, 1980.

SOURCE NOTES BY CHAPTER

PROLOGUE—THE UNCROWNED KING OF CANADA
1. "Mackenzie King genuinely": Pickersgill, *TMKR*, Vol. 1, p. 10.
2. "history of his": Ibid., viii.
3. "Mackenzie King was": Neatby, *WLMK*, Vol. II, p. 408.
4. "consulted spiritual advisers": Turnbull to Jean Bruce, CBC-*DBY*, March 13, 1973, FR #292, transcript p. 1.
5. "It contributes nothing": Esberey, *KOTHS*, p. 132.
6. "fully appreciated the": Stacey, *AVDL*, p. 198.
7. "Never did he": Ibid.
8. "spirits did not": Ibid., p. 199.
9. "Truly he will": Scott and Smith, p. 28.
10. "King operated mainly": Hardy, *MKOC*, p. 287.
11. "King thought that": Ibid., p. 337.
12. "numerous occasions": Rockefeller to David Scrivens, CBD-*DBY*, January 22, 1973, FR #265, transcript p. 1.
13. "Father had no": Ibid., p. 5.
14. "catlike in his": Hardy, *MKOC*, p. 162.
15. "It was all": Blumer, *FO*, Part Three, p. 27.
16. "over the little": Stacey, *CHR*, LXI, 4, 1980, p. 502.
17. "marvellous host and": Pickersgill, *TMKR*, Vol. 1., p. 4.
18. "He was a": MacDonald to Robert McKenzie, CBC-*DBY*, July 10, 1973, FR #11, transcript p. 3.
19. "King's tremendous asset": Sinclair to Cameron Graham, CBC-*DBY*, April 24, 1972, FR #64, p. 1.
20. "Mr. King, how": Ibid., pp. 2,3.
21. "What would the": Hardy, *MKOC*, p. 370.
22. "All industry and": Pickersgill to Jean Bruce, CBC-*DBY*, February 15, 1973, FR #271, transcript p. 1.
23. "For every story": Hardy, *MKOC*, p. 163.
24. "The first and": Hutchison, *TIC*, p. 7.
25. "Did you have": O'Leary to Larry Zolf, CBC-*DBY*, March 22, 1972, FR #57, transcript p. 1.

PRELUDE—THE DIVINE MISSION
1. "one of the": Stacey, *CHR*, LXI, 4, 1980, p. 512.
2. "without the help": Bryan and Murphy, *TWS*, p. 345.
3. "distorted all King's": Hutchison, *TIC*, p. 225.
4. "The Supreme Court": Shirer, *BD*, p. 13.

5. "like the headquarters": Speer, *ITTR*, p. 34.
6. "bound to be": King, *KD*, June 29, 1937.
7. "He smiled very": Ibid.
8. "Looking back over": Ibid.
9. "never saw anyone": Toland, *AH*, p. 27.
10. "was in all": Hutchison, *TIC*, p. 39.
11. "You will succeed": Stacey, *CHR*, LXI 4, 1980, p. 503.
12. "distinctly a mystic": King, *KD*, June 29, 1937.
13. "embroidering the impressions": Stacey, *CHR*, LXI 4, 1980, p. 512.
14. "simple sort of": et seq., Hutchison, *TIC*, p. 225-6.
15. "Get out of": Hardy, *MKOC*, p. 166.
16. "the heart of": Eayrs, *IDOC*, p. 70.
17. "thought we should": Pickersgill to Jean Bruce, CBC-*DBY*, February 15, 1973, FR #269, transcript p. 6.
18. "A greater leader": Hutchison to Larry Zolf, CBC-*DBY*, May 11, 1971, FR #15, transcript p. 4.
19. "number of Canadian": Eayrs, *IDOC*, p. 77.
20. "to practise appeasement": Ibid., p. 78.
21. "the Prime Minister": Ibid.
22. "the craziest of": et seq., Stacey, *AVDL*, p. 190.
23. "I like to": Esberey, *KOTHS*, p.72.
24. "cut your throat": O'Leary to Larry Zolf, CBC-*DBY*, March 22, 1972, FR #57, transcript p. 2.

CHAPTER ONE—TREACHERY IN QUEBEC

1. "free as a": King, *KD*, September 15, 1939.
2. "really in good": Ibid.
3. "a second Hitler": Ibid., September 27, 1939.
4. "would be outstanding": Ibid.
5. "did not hesitate": Black, *Duplessis*, p. 660.
6. "At least it": Hutchison, *TIC*, p. 261.
7. "a thorough gangster": King, *KD*, September 25, 1939.
8. "Gregarious and aloof": Black, *Duplessis*, p. 660.
9. "He believed in": et seq., Ludington to Brian Nolan, CBC-*DBY*, November 28, 1972, FR #136, transcript p. 4.
10. "He was a": Ibid., FR #137, pp. 3,4.
11. "believed in only": Black, *Duplessis*, p. 679.
12. "one-night stands": Ibid., p. 218.
13. "Madame, I have": Ibid., p. 681.
14. "A distinguished looking": Ibid., p. 661.

15. "What does it": et seq., Ludington to Brian Nolan, CBC-*DBY*, November 28, 1972, FR #136, transcript pp. 8, 9.
16. "You know, my": et seq., Casgrain to Jean Bruce, CBC-*DBY*, January 19, 1973, FR #258, transcript pp. 5, 6.
17. "My war experiences": Power, *APP*, p. 43.
18. "he might break": King, *KD*, September 19, 1939.
19. "If Chubby Power": Power, *APP*, p. 54.
20. "had affection almost": Pickersgill, *TMKR*, Vol. I, p. 8.
21. "was perhaps Canadian": Black, *Duplessis*, p. 207.
22. "It heard from": Hutchison, *TIC*, p. 263.
23. "persons who might": Power, *APP*, p. 128.
24. "their financial representatives": Ibid., p. 348.
25. "Perhaps because all": Ibid.
26. "wildly hilarious government": Black, *Duplessis*, p. 218.
27. "as far in": King, *KD*, October 25, 1939.
28. "tremendously pleased and": Ibid., October 26, 1939.
29. "or some other": Ibid.
30. "It is a": King, *KD*, October 25, 1939.
31. "In retrospect it": Hutchison, *TIC*, p. 262.
32. "We shall have": Black, *Duplessis*, p. 214.

CHAPTER TWO—TREASON IN ONTARIO

1. "a delicious Christmas": King, *KD*, December 25, 1939.
2. "the cause of": Ibid., December 16, 1939.
3. "had few qualms": English, Stubbs (Granatstein), *MK:WTD*, p. 174.
4. "what the New": King, *KD*, December 31, 1939.
5. "sound a clear": et seq., McKenty, *MH*, pp. 208, 209.
6. "was ever sure": et seq., Pickersgill to Jean Bruce, CBC-*DBY*, February 15, 1973, FR #270, transcript pp. 5, 6.
7. "not of the": McKenty, *MH*, p. 34.
8. "friendliness and folksiness": Ibid., p. 59.
9. "the most diabolical": Ibid., p. 62.
10. "He wore a": Ibid., p. 182.
11. "Is your wife": et seq., Hume to Larry Zolf, CBC-*DBY*, December 4, 1972, FR #159, transcript pp. 7, 8.
12. "well-Primed Minister": McKenty, *MH*, p. 236.
13. "shocking betrayal of": et seq., King, *KD*, January 18 and 19, 1940.
14. "While not infallible": English, Stubbs (Granatstein) *MK:WTD*, p. 175.
15. "certainly a real": King, *KD*, January 25, 1940.
16. "was some doubt": Power, *APP*, p. 353.
17. "that King must": et seq., McKenty, *MH*, p. 211.

18. "had taken leave": et seq., Bell to Jean Bruce, CBC-*DBY*, September 28, 1973, FR # 393, transcript p. 5.
19. "to gauge public": et seq., Stevens to Larry Zolf, CBC-*DBY*, May 10, 1971, FR #2, transcript p. 4.
20. "nothing but political": McKenty, *MH*, p. 213.
21. "that this was": Evans, *JGATNFB*, p. 74.
22. "This war demands": Pickersgill, *TMKR*, Vol. 1, p. 69.
23. "We really cleaned": King, *KD*, March 26, 1940.
24. "wanted Mitch to": McKenty, *MH*, p. 218.
25. "Just a note": Ibid.

CHAPTER THREE—FOES AND A FRIEND

1. "love of Jesus": et seq., *Canadian Forum*, December 1939, Vol. IX, pp. 269, 343.
2. "the desirability of": King, *KD*, January 18, 1940.
3. "generally fed up": et seq., Power, *APP*, pp. 350, 351.
4. "disloyal remarks": et seq., *Canadian Forum*, September, 1940, Vol. XX, p. 173.
5. "Oh, you've come": et seq., Ludington to Brian Nolan, CBC-*DBY*, November 28, 1972, FR #138, transcript p. 5.
6. "It thus authorized": Stacey, *SYOW*, p. 82.
7. "Type it out": Ibid., transcript p. 3.
8. "It is unequivocally": *Gazette*, August 3, 1940.
9. "Hanson's questions clearly": King, *KD*, Aug. 5, 1940.
10. "I think he": Ludington to Brian Nolan, CBC-*DBY*, November 28, 1972, FR #138, transcript p. 4.
11. "The popularity of": Martin, *TPATPM*, p. 117.
12. "I give to you": Ibid., p. 127.
13. "We are having": et seq., Hardy, *MKOC*, p. 176.

CHAPTER FOUR—DEATH IN THE ORIENT

1. "a blinky-eyed": Manchester, *AC*, p. 319.
2. "tree to tree": Manchester, *TGATD*, p. 265.
3. "Never let the": Manchester, *AC*, p. 323.
4. "The Japanese may": Manchester, *TGATD*, p. 263.
5. "The Canadians who": Vincent, *NRW*, p. 35.
6. "If Japan goes": Ibid., p. 11.
7. "Canada could probably": Ibid., p. 26.
8. "there have been": Ibid., p. 29.

9. "that the Canadian": Ibid., p. 33.
10. "They had no": Stacey, *TCA*, p. 288.
11. "Did the odds": Vincent, *NRW*, p. 94.
12. "a help to": King, *KD*, January 22, 1942.
13. "Its wording really": Ibid., June 4, 1942.
14. "In the case": Vincent, *NRW*, p. 39.
15. "had expected war": Pickersgill, *TMKR*, Vol. 1, p. 296.
16. "Duff, no matter": Vincent, *NRW*, p. 223.
17. "sullied his victory": Stacey, *TCA*, p. 287.

CHAPTER FIVE—THE ENEMY THAT NEVER WAS

1. "The Chinamen and": Berger, *FFHRADIC*, p. 103.
2. "what Canadian history": Abella and Troper, *NITM*, p. x.
3. "open its doors": Ibid., p. 64.
4. "whenever he was": Berger, *FFHRADIC*, p. 113.
5. "The competition for": Ibid., p. 113.
6. "At that time": Green to Peter Trueman, December 2, 1976.
7. "At a stroke": Berger, *FFHRADIC*, p. 107.
8. "I feel, too": King, *KD*, February 23, 1942.
9. "They were herded": Tucker to Brian Nolan, December 6, 1976.
10. "A person had": Nakayama to Brian Nolan, October (no date), 1976.
11. "Concern for the": Pope to Jean Bruce, CBC-*DBY*, July 31, 1973, FR #366, transcript p. 4.
12. "The soldiers of": Evans, *JGATNFB*, p. 216.
13. "The United States": Berger, *FFHRADIC*, p. 114.
14. "King's policy would": Ibid., pp. 114, 115.
15. "It's one of": Pickersgill to Jean Bruce, CBC-*DBY*, February 16, 1973, FR #280, transcript p. 4.
16. "the white races": Adachi, *TETNW*, p. 367.
17. "to the edge": Hutchison, *TIC*, p. 297.

Author's Note: Abella's and Troper's *None Is Too Many*, and Adachi's *The Enemy That Never Was*, remain the definitive works about Jewish refugee immigration in Canada, and the story of the plight of Japanese Canadians respectively. Further sources for this chapter were transcripts and research notes compiled for the documentary *Tides of War, The Story of Japanese-Canadians During World War II*, produced and directed by the author, and co-written with Peter Trueman, for the *Global Television Network*. This one-hour documentary was broadcast April 3, 1977.

CHAPTER SIX—KING'S NEMESIS

1. "God be with": et seq., King, *KD*, June 14, 15, 1941.
2. "sick at heart": Ibid., November 8, 1941.
3. "the most reactionary": et seq., Hutchison, *TIC*, p. 298.
4. "Victorian belief in": et seq., English, *AM(TC)*, pp. 4, 5.
5. "was pestered, ridiculed": et seq., Ibid., p. 34.
6. "Meighen had command": Hume to Larry Zolf, CBC-*DBY*, December 4, 1972, FR #161, transcript p. 2.
7. "I am getting": King, *KD*, November 6, 1941.
8. "He was horrified,": Hutchison to Larry Zolf, CBC-*DBY*, May 11, 1971, FR #16, transcript p. 4.
9. "he was a": Bell to Jean Bruce, CBC-*DBY*, September 28, 1973, FR #393, transcript p. 6.
10. "Let us consider": et seq., Vincent, *NRW*, p. 220.
11. "the most dastardly": McKenty, *MH*, p. 237.
12. "so amateurish and": King, *KD*, March 19, 1942.
13. "I would just": Graham, *AM*, p. 110.
14. "One shudders to": et seq., Ibid., pp. 122, 128, 129.
15. "I felt tonight": et seq., King, *KD*, Feb. 9, 1942.
16. "I'll be taking": et seq., Mrs. Arthur Meighen to Geoff Scott, CBC-*DBY*, March 19, 1972, FR #10, transcript p. 3.
17. "He despised him.": Maxwell Meighen to Cameron Graham, CBC-*DBY*, December 12, 1972, FR #182, transcript p. 2.

CHAPTER SEVEN—FIRST CRISIS AVERTED

1. "would not give": et seq., Hardy, *MKOC*, p. 141.
2. "written in King's": et seq., Hutchison, *TIC*, p. 305.
3. "factor was racial": et seq., King, *KD*, April 27, 1942.
4. "was seeking to": et seq., Ibid., April 28, 1942.
5. "not necessarily conscription": Ibid., June 9, 1942.
6. "you don't need": Pickersgill to Jean Bruce, *CBC-DBY*, February 15, 1973, FR #267, transcript p. 8.
7. "that nothing was": Pickersgill, *TMKR*, Vol. 1, p. 5.
8. "I gave Mr.": et seq., Pickersgill to Sigmund Brouwer, 1987 (no date).
9. "Not necessarily conscription": Toronto *Star*, April 28, 1942.
10. "than all the": Pickersgill, *TMKR*, Vol. 1, p. 386.

CHAPTER EIGHT—THE SAILOR'S WAR

1. "probably the most": Boutilier (J.H.W. Knox) *RCNIR*, p. 110.
2. "young RCN officers": Ibid., p. xxiv.

3. "Unused to the": Lamb, *OTTR*, p. 32.
4. "What ship?": et seq., Ibid., p. 35.
5. "fear of heights": Garner, *ODTAA*, p. 58.
6. "That was quite": McLennan to Brian Nolan, February 3, 1988.
7. "everyone knew whose": Lamb, *OTTR*, p. 27.
8. "RCN corvettes have": Boutilier (Marc Milner), *RCNIR*, p. 163.
9. "eighty per cent": German, *CDQ*, Special Issue, December 1985–January 1986, p. 22.
10. "cycled through a": Ibid.
11. "I have bad": et seq., King, *KD*, September 27, 1943.
12. "Her voice was": et seq., Ibid., September 27, 28, and October 1, 1943.
13. "I stressed the": Ibid., May 13, 1943.

CHAPTER NINE—THE AIRMAN'S WAR

1. "Tell me about": Speer to Brian Nolan, May 29, 1976.
2. "was speaking to": et seq., King, *KD*, December 16 and 17, 1939.
3. "clear political advantages": Douglas, *TCOANAF*, p. 191.
4. "King was reluctant": Ibid., pp. 191, 192.
5. "his blunt talk": et seq., Roberts, *CD*, pp. 5, 4.
6. "I didn't ask": Bothwell and Kilbourn, *CDH*, p. 137.
7. "If any of": et seq., Roberts, *CD*, pp. 108, 109.
8. "Minister was little": et seq., Power, *APP*, pp. 206, 207, 189.
9. "gargled with gin": Leroy Prinz to Brian Nolan, September 9, 1974.
10. "mugs": Power, *APP*, p. 221.
11. "a major contributor": Douglas, *TCOANAF*, p. 192.
12. "And that": Patrick Watson to Speer, May 29, 1976.*

---

*Dining that night in Berlin with Speer were the author, Patrick Watson and William R. Cunningham, at that time the vice-president of News, of the Global Television Network which had commissioned the documentary on Speer called *The Last Nazi*. Watson and Nolan, who had just finished two years' work on a history of flight series for the CBC called *Flight: The Passionate Affair*, still had freshly in their minds considerable facts about the BCATP. At one point Speer asked, somewhat suspiciously, how they were so familiar with the details of the plan. Speer seemed satisfied with their explanation.

Author's Note: Readers interested in knowing more about the BCATP are directed to read *The Plan: Memories of the British Commonwealth Air Training Plan* by James N. Williams. His colourful oral history is a delight to read.

13. "produced a scale": Middlebrook, Martin and Everitt, *TBCWD*, p. 11.
14. "The war situation": King, *KD*, March 5, 1945.

CHAPTER TEN—THE SOLDIER'S WAR

1. "the responsible military": et seq., Robertson, *TSATGD*, pp. 140, 144, 141.
2. "I still have": King, *KD*, August 21, 1942.
3. "If I had": Robertson, *TSATGD*, p. xi.
4. "About a quarter": Roy, *CDQ*, p. 40.
5. "one of the": Stacey, *TCA*, p. 235.

CHAPTER ELEVEN—THE DESPERATE SUMMER

1. "were too green": Smythe (Young), *CS:IYCBEITA*, p. 160.
2. "The reinforcement situation": Ibid., p. 168.
3. "green, inexperienced and": Ibid., p. 167.
4. "The whole thing": King, *KD*, August 8, 1944.
5. "Whether he disliked": Turnbull to Jean Bruce, CBC-*DBY*, March 13, 1973, FR #291, transcript p. 4.
6. "One of the": Pickersgill to Jean Bruce, CBC-*DBY*, February 15, 1973, FR #272, transcript p. 7.
7. "fighting with all": et seq., Turnbull to Jean Bruce, CBC-*DBY*, March 13, 1973, FR #291, p. 3.
8. "It was a": et seq., O'Leary to Larry Zolf, CBC-*DBY*, March 22, 1972, Fr #57, transcript pp. 10, 11.
9. "This incredible attention": Sinclair to Cameron Graham, CBC-*DBY*, March 24, 1972, FR #62, transcript p. 10.
10. "the lightest heart": King, *KD*, September 23, 1944.
11. "You court-martial": Smythe (Young), *CS:IYCBEITA*, pp. 169, 170.
12. "Do you want": Malone, *AWIF*, p. 146.
13. "an act of": Whitaker, D., and S., *TOW*, p. 228.
14. "faced the finest": et seq., Hastings, *ODDATBFN*, p. 315.
15. "alarmist cables": Whitaker, D., and S., *TOW*, p. 214.
16. "we had plenty": King, *KD*, August 3, 1944.
17. "[t]his was the": Whitaker, D., and S., *TOW*, p. 216.
18. "of this travesty": Ibid., p. 216.
19. "The enemy": Ibid., p. 375.
20. "We had only": Ibid., p. 217.
21. "an unfortunate and": Dunkelman, *DA*, p. 123.

22. "About the standard": et seq., Whitaker, D., and S., *TOW*, pp. 232, 233.
23. "was the brightest": et seq., Foster, *MOG*, p. 340.
24. "taken as a": et seq., Whitaker, D., and S., *TOW*, pp. 230, 231.
25. "There was a": Malone, *AWIF*, pp. 145, 147.
26. "occasioned me great": et seq., King, *KD*, October 13, 1944.
27. "too fanciful even": Hutchison, *TIC*, p. 343.

CHAPTER TWELVE—THE STORM BURSTS

1. "After a pause": King, *KD*, October 18, 1944.
2. "was perfectly indifferent": Ibid.
3. "these burdens to": Ibid.
4. "with the little": Ibid.
5. "be a source": et seq., Ibid.
6. "Should Ralston press": Ibid., October 19, 1944.
7. "In the meantime": et seq., Ibid.
8. "I asked Stuart": Ibid.
9. "There is something": Ibid.
10. "Little does he": Ibid., October 25, 1944.
11. "His reply": Ibid., October 26, 1944.
12. "He wasn't the": Pickersgill to Jean Bruce, CBC-*DBY*, February 15, 1975, FR #273, transcript pp. 9, 10.
13. "I asked him": Pope to Jean Bruce, Ibid., July 31, 1973, FR #369, transcript p. 2.
14. "I outlined to": King, *KD*, October 31, 1944.

CHAPTER THIRTEEN—BETRAYAL

1. "I then said": King, *KD*, November 1, 1944.
2. "our men and": The *Evening Citizen*, November 6, 1944.
3. "Give the Zombies": Ibid., November 7, 1944.
4. "The glory of": The *Globe*, November 9, 1944.
5. "was not as": King, *KD*, November 14, 1944.
6. "felt very depressed": King, *KD*, November 21, 1944.
7. "I have terrible": Hutchison, *TIC*, p. 374.
8. "that very day": Pope to Jean Bruce, CBC-*DBY*, July 31, 1973, FR #369, transcript p. 4.
9. "But . . . a lot": Turnbull to Jean Bruce, Ibid., March 13, 1973, FR #292, transcript p. 7.
10. "I desire to read": *Hansard*, November 23, 1944.

EPILOGUE

1. "Thank God": King, *KD*, May 7, 1945.
2. "I kept going": Ibid., June 16, 1945.
3. "patriotism rose above": Hutchison to Larry Zolf, CBC-*DBY*, May 11, 1971, FR #15, transcript p. 6.
4. "It lies peacefully": King, *KD*, August 10, 1948.

BIBLIOGRAPHY

BOOKS

Abella, Irving, and Troper, Harold. *None Is Too Many*. Toronto: Lester & Orpen Dennys, 1982.

Adachi, Ken. *The Enemy That Never Was*. Toronto: McClelland and Stewart Limited, 1976.

Allen, Ralph. *Ordeal by Fire*. New York: Doubleday & Company, Inc., 1961.

Berger, Thomas R. *Fragile Freedoms, Human Rights and Dissent in Canada*. Toronto/Vancouver: Clarke, Irwin & Company Limited, 1981.

Black, Conrad. *Duplessis*. Toronto: McClelland and Stewart Limited, 1977.

Boutilier, James B., ed. *RCN in Retrospect, 1910–1968*. Vancouver and London: The University of British Columbia Press, 1982.

Bryan, J., III, and Murphy, Charles J.V. *The Windsor Story*. New York: William Morrow and Company, Inc., 1979.

Butcher, Harry C., Capt., USNR. *My Three Years with Eisenhower*. New York: Simon and Schuster, 1946.

Calder, Nigel. *The English Channel*. New York: Viking Penguin Inc., 1986.

Cederberg, Fred. *The Long Road Home*. Toronto: General Publishing Co. Ltd., 1984.

Bothwell, Robert, and Kilbourn, William. *C.D. Howe*. Toronto: McClelland and Stewart Limited, 1979.

Churchill, Winston S. *Closing the Ring*. Boston: Houghton Mifflin Company, 1951.

———. *The Gathering Storm*. Boston: Houghton Mifflin Company, 1948.

———. *The Grand Alliance*. Boston: Houghton Mifflin Company, 1950.

———. *The Hinge of Fate*. Boston: Houghton Mifflin Company, 1950.

———. *Their Finest Hour*. Boston: Houghton Mifflin Company, 1949.

———. *Triumph and Tragedy*. Boston: Houghton Mifflin Company, 1953.

Connell, Evan S. *Son of the Morning Star*. San Francisco: North Point Press, 1984.

Dawson, R. MacGregor. *The Conscription Crisis of 1944*. Toronto: University of Toronto Press, 1961.

Douglas, W.A.B. *The Creation of a National Air Force, The Official History of The Royal Canadian Air Force Volume II*. Ottawa and Toronto: University of Toronto Press in co-operation with the Department of National Defence and the Canadian Government Publishing Centre, Supply and Services Canada, 1986.

Dunkelman, Ben. *Dual Allegiance*. Toronto: Macmillan of Canada, 1976.

Easton, Alan. *50 North*. Toronto: The Ryerson Press, 1963.

Eayrs, James. *In Defence of Canada, Appeasement and Rearmament*. Toronto: University of Toronto Press, 1965.

English, John. *Arthur Meighen* (The Canadians). Don Mills, Ont.: Fitzhenry and Whiteside Limited, 1977.

Esberey, Joy E. *Knight of the Holy Spirit: A Study of William Lyon Mackenzie King*. Toronto: University of Toronto Press, 1980.

Evans, Gary. *John Grierson and the National Film Board: The Politics of Wartime Propaganda*. Toronto: University of Toronto Press, 1984.

English, John, and Stubbs, J.O., eds. *Mackenzie King: Widening the Debate*. Toronto: Macmillan Company of Canada, 1977.

Foster, Tony. *Meeting of Generals*. Agincourt, Ont.: Methuen Publications, 1986.

Gann, Ernest K. *A Hostage to Fortune*. New York: Alfred A. Knopf, 1978.

———. *Fate Is the Hunter*. New York: Simon and Schuster, Inc., 1961.

Garner, Hugh. *One Damn Thing After Another*. Toronto: McGraw-Hill Ryerson Limited, 1973.

Graham, Roger. *Arthur Meighen*, Vol. III, Toronto/Vancouver: Clarke, Irwin & Company, 1965.

Granatstein, J.L. *Canada's War: The Politics of the Mackenzie King Government, 1939–1945*. Toronto: Oxford University Press, 1975.

———. *Mackenzie King: His Life and World*. Toronto: McGraw-Hill Ryerson Limited, 1977.

———. *The Ottawa Men: The Civil Service Mandarins, 1935–1957*. Toronto: Oxford University Press, 1982.

Hardy, Reginald H. *Mackenzie King of Canada*. Toronto: Oxford University Press, 1949.

Hastings, Max. *Overlord D-Day, June 6, 1944*. New York: Simon and Schuster, 1984.

How, Douglas, ed. *Canadians at War. Volumes 1 & 2*. Montreal: Reader's Digest Association (Canada) Ltd., 1969.

Hutchison, Bruce. *The Incredible Canadian*. Toronto: Longmans, Green and Company, 1952.

———. *Mr. Prime Minister*. Don Mills, Ont.: Longmans Canada Limited, 1964.

———. *The Unfinished Country: To Canada with Love and Some Misgivings*. Vancouver: Douglas & McIntyre Ltd., 1985.

King, William Lyon Mackenzie. *The Mackenzie King Diaries, 1932–1949. Microfiche Edition*. Toronto: University of Toronto Press, 1980.

Knightley, Philip, and Simpson, Colin. *The Secret Lives of Lawrence of Arabia*. London: Thomas Nelson and Sons Ltd., 1969.

Lamb, James B. *On The Triangle Run*. Toronto: Macmillan of Canada, 1986.

———. *The Corvette Navy: True Stories from Canada's Atlantic War*. Toronto: The Macmillan Company of Canada, (no date).

Lynch, Thomas G. *Canada's Flowers: History of the Corvettes of Canada, 1939–1945*. Halifax: Nimbus Publishing Limited, 1981.

Malone, Richard S. *A World in Flames, 1944–1945*. Don Mills, Ont.: Collins Publishers, 1984.

Manchester, William. *American Caesar: Douglas MacArthur 1880–1964*. Boston: Little, Brown and Company, 1977.

———. *American Caesar*. New York: Dell Publishing Co., Inc., 1978.

———. *The Glory and the Dream: A Narrative History of America, 1932–1972*. Boston: Little, Brown and Company, 1974.

Martin, Lawrence. *The Presidents and the Prime Ministers*. Toronto: Doubleday Canada Limited, 1982.

McCall-Newman, Christina. *Grits: An Intimate Portrait of the Liberal Party*. Toronto: Macmillan of Canada, 1982.

McDougall, Robert L., ed. *Canada's Past and Present: A Dialogue, Volume 5*. Toronto: Carleton University in association with University of Toronto Press, 1965.

McKenty, Neil. *Mitch Hepburn*. Toronto: McClelland and Stewart Limited, 1967.

Middlebrook, Martin, and Everitt, Chris. *The Bomber Command War Diaries: An Operational Reference Book, 1939–1945*. New York: Viking Penguin Inc., 1985.

Mowat, Farley. *And No Birds Sang*. Toronto: McClelland and Stewart, 1979.

———. *The Regiment*. Toronto: McClelland and Stewart, 1955.

Parrish, Thomas, ed. *The Simon and Schuster Encyclopedia of World War II*. New York: Simon and Schuster, 1978.

Peden, Murray. *A Thousand Shall Fall*. Stittsville, Ontario: Canada's Wings, 1979.

Pickersgill, J.W. *The Mackenzie King Record, Volume 1, 1939–1944*. Toronto: University of Toronto Press, 1960.

Pickersgill, J.W., and Forster, D.F. *The Mackenzie King Record, Volume 2, 1944–1945*. Toronto: University of Toronto Press, 1968.

———. *The Mackenzie King Record, Volume 3, 1945–1946*. Toronto: University of Toronto Press, 1970.

Power, C.G., and Ward, Norman, ed. *A Party Politician: The Memoirs of Chubby Power*. Toronto: The Macmillan Company of Canada Limited, 1966.

Rhodes, Richard. *The Making of the Atomic Bomb*. New York: Simon and Schuster, 1986.

Ritchie, Charles. *The Siren Years: A Canadian Diplomat Abroad, 1937–1945*. Toronto: Macmillan of Canada, 1974.

Roberts, Leslie C.D. *The Life and Times of Clarence Decatur Howe*. Toronto: Clarke, Irwin & Company Limited, 1957.

Robertson, Terence. *The Shame and the Glory — Dieppe*. Toronto: McClelland and Stewart Limited, 1967 (first paperback edition).

Scott, F.R., and Smith, A.J.M. *The Blasted Pine*. Toronto: Macmillan of Canada, 1957.

Shirer, William L. *Twentieth Century Journey: A Memoir of a Life and the Times, Volume II, The Nightmare Years, 1930-1940*. Boston: Little, Brown and Company, 1984.

——. *Berlin Diary*. New York: Alfred A. Knopf, Inc., 1940.

——. *The Rise and Fall of the Third Reich: A History of Nazi Germany*. New York: Simon and Schuster, Inc., 1959.

Smythe, Conn, with Young, Scott. *Conn Smyth: If You Can't Beat 'em in the Alley*. Toronto: McClelland and Stewart Limited, 1981.

Speer, Albert. *Inside the Third Reich*. London: Weidenfeld and Nicolson, 1970.

Stacey, C.P. *A Very Double Life: The Private World of Mackenzie King*. Toronto: The Macmillan Company of Canada, 1976.

——. *Arms, Men and Governments: The War Policies of Canada, 1939-1945*. Ottawa: Minister of National Defence, 1970.

——. *Six Years of War*. Ottawa: Minister of National Defence, 1966.

——. *The Canadian Army, 1939-1945: An Official Historical Summary*. Ottawa: King's Printer, 1948.

Stratford, Philip, ed. *André Laurendeau: Witness for Quebec*. Toronto: Macmillan of Canada, 1973.

Swettenham, John. *McNaughton, Volume 2, 1939-1943*. Toronto: The Ryerson Press, 1969.

——. *McNaughton, Volume 3, 1944-1966*. Toronto: The Ryerson Press, 1969.

Toland, John. *Adolf Hitler*. New York: Doubleday & Company, Inc., 1976.

Vincent, Carl. *No Reason Why: The Canadian Hong Kong Tragedy — an Examination*. Stittsville, Ont.: Canada's Wings, Inc., 1981.

Whitaker, W. Denis, and Whitaker, Shelagh. *Tug of War, The Canadian Victory That Opened Antwerp*. Toronto: Stoddart Publishing, 1984.

Williams, James N. *The Plan: Memories of the British Commonwealth Air Training Plan*. Stittsville, Ont.: Canada's Wings, Inc., 1984.

Young, Peter, Brigadier. *The World Almanac Book of World War II*. New York: World Almanac Publications, 1981.

FICTION

Garner, Hugh. *Storm Below*. Don Mills, Ont.: Collins Publishers, 1949.

PERIODICALS, ARTICLES, ETC.

Blumer, Ronald. "Fixed Obsession". Six-part research paper for the National Film Board of Canada, for the six-hour television series, *King Chronicle*, broadcast March 1988, CBC-TV, and produced by Donald Brittain and Adam Symansky.

German, A.B., Commander, RCN (ret.). "Canada's Navy 1910 to 1985." Ottawa: *Canadian Defence Quarterly*, December 1985.

———. "Fighting The Submarine — A Chronology". Ottawa: *Canadian Defence Quarterly*, December 1985.

Rigby, Vincent G. "Air Marshal Harold ('Gus') Edwards and the Canadianization of the RCAF Overseas, 1941–43." *Canadian Defence Quarterly*, Winter 1987.

Roy, R.H. "Morale in the Canadian Army in Canada During the Second World War." *Canadian Defence Quarterly*, August 1986.

Stacey, C.P. "The Divine Mission: Mackenzie King and Hitler." *Canadian Historical Review*, LXI, 4, 1980.

INDEX